Navigating the Toggled Term: Preparing Secondary Educators for Navigating Fall 2020 and Beyond

By: Matthew Rhoads, Ed.D.

Table of Contents

Dedication

I dedicate this book to all educators who are tirelessly working to ensure students continuously learning throughout the COVID-19 crisis. Living in a family full of teachers, we talk about education on a daily basis. We dialogue and reflect on how to create the best outcomes we can for students. I want to thank my wife for consistently challenging my ideas, as well as my mentors, who always give me thoughtful feedback. This is also for you. Also, I want to thank my parents for inspiring me and always providing me feedback on my work. Lastly, thanks to my sister, Anna Rhoads, for creating the cover and back cover graphics. It is impressive work that illustrates what this book represents!

Introduction

Education has been rattled. With the COVID-19 (Coronavirus) crisis transforming all aspects of daily life, schools have had to adjust significantly in order to provide students with instruction. All face-to-face instruction has been canceled. As a result, online instruction has become one of the most sought-after forms of instruction during this time. Districts, schools, and teachers had to mobilize quickly to create online classes in a matter of weeks for their students with varying results.

Questions loom as to what schools will look like once state governors give districts and schools the green light to start developing and refining plans for a fall 2020 initial reopening and navigating the 2020-2021 school year. Ultimately, reopening schools has become one of the major phases of restoring the economy. Still, it will require vast resources and innovative thinking to make them a safe environment for the short-term and long-term once again for students, teachers, and staff.

Schools must reassess how instruction will take place with social distancing protocols in place on campus. Simultaneously, they must think into the future with the looming fear of having to close down once again if the second wave of COVID-19 hits in the fall and winter. This could result in what we can call a "toggled term" for K-12 education. The toggled term was initially coined by Bryan Alexander, an education futurist who alluded to this happening for higher education during the fall of 2020. Now, it seems inevitable that this "toggled term" will also be the reality in K-12 education for the foreseeable future (Alexander, 2020). Thus, as schools may reopen to face-to-face instruction in some capacity and begin easing into a blended learning model over time, they may have to be closed once again and return to online learning.

The Toggled Term for K-12 Education		
Blended Learning Face to Face and Asynchronous Online Instruction	**The "Toggle"**	**Fully Online Instruction**
• Face to face and online instruction • Social Distancing • Hyper Hygiene Practices • Staggered Scheduling	Opening/Closing of Physical Campus's (Dictated by Local Health Conditions) **Note:** Instruction is always occurring ← →	• Online synchronous and asynchronous instruction only • Temporary until health conditions improve • All instructional platforms and content will always be online just in case a toggle occurs where schools have to close facilities

Figure 1. The Toggled Term for K-12 Education

All over the education landscape, especially regarding the outpouring of tutorials, commentary, and analysis on how to use edtech and how instructional strategies can be integrated with edtech tools for online instruction (Ferlazzo, 2020; Ferdig & Kennedy, 2018). Further, there has been massive support on Twitter by both teachers and administrators to develop professional learning communities to build capacity in teaching students in an online educational setting. Thus, based on this explosion of content and collaboration, it is evident that K-12 educators have learned an extensive amount of knowledge on edtech integration over the course of the spring 2020 semester with the advent of online distance learning. However, even with this growth in educator capacity, we see two major issues arising from online learning. First, according to publications found in Forbes (2020), The Hechinger Report (2020), and the Association of California School Administrators EdCal (2020), equity and access have become ever more present as online instruction has become prevalent during this crisis. Many students do not have access to high-quality internet and devices to help them participate in online learning. Second, teachers of all grade levels have to continue to learn how to use educational technology as well as integrating technology with blended learning models at a rapid pace. Ultimately, this will provide a synthesis of instruction to students online in addition to some form of face to face instruction once schools reopen. Due to varying amounts of training and resources provided to teachers, there are gaps in the knowledge of the education technology tools. Additionally, gaps exist in incorporating instructional strategies to make the edtech tools effective in asynchronous and synchronous online and blended learning classroom educational settings.

Policymakers, educational leaders, and teachers find themselves in a precarious position as they are now tasked to reopen schools. With what we now know about what happened during the advent of online learning in spring 2020, educators can develop in-depth plans to be utilized before schools reopen in the late summer and early fall.

Organization of this Book

The purpose of this book is to help all secondary educators to build their capacity in three ways: 1) Solidifying Your District and Schools Edtech and Online Instructional Infrastructure, 2) Maximizing Synchronous Instruction, Parent & Student Engagement and Communication, Differentiated Instruction, and Navigating Special Education, and 3) Navigating Fall 2020 and Beyond, Reopening Schools, Learning Models that can Toggle, and Continued Professional Development. These three major areas make up Parts 1, 2, and 3 of this book, which creates the foundation for secondary educators to navigate many of the instructional challenges presented by a toggled term. Finally, to round out the book, Part 4 will act as the book's conclusion that will further elaborate on how to best navigate the toggled term by providing an organizational and cultural framework to allow secondary schools to toggle back and forth between face to face and online instruction for the foreseeable future. To complete the conclusion, the future of K-12 education, as we know it in the post-COVID world, will be previewed.

Part 1. Solidifying Your Schools Edtech and Online Instructional Infrastructure

1. Selecting Edtech Tools for your Online and Blended Learning Classroom
2. Edtech Tools to Get You Started with Your Online and Blended Teaching! Start Now!
3. Steps to Building Your Online Classroom for K-12 Educators
4. Implementing Instructional Strategies and Lesson Plans with Edtech for your Online Classrooms

Part 2. Maximizing Synchronous Instruction, Parent & Student Engagement and Communication, Differentiated Instruction, and Navigating Special Education

5. Maximizing Live Synchronous Class Sessions and Google Meet – Strategies to Help Bolster Your Students Online Learning
6. Student and Parental Engagement for Online Learning - Building Community Online through Edtech
7. Differentiated Instruction - Online Instruction for Special Education and English Language Learners

Part 3. Navigating Fall 2020 and Beyond, Reopening Schools, Learning Models that can Toggle, and Continued Professional Development.

Part 4. Conclusion - Navigating the Future of Secondary Education Within a Toggled Term

Each section builds upon each other because we cannot serve our students in a toggled term unless online instruction is the foundation for reopening schools. Remember, at a moment's notice; we can suddenly go back to solely online instruction if a fall second wave of COVID-19 makes it too dangerous for students and teachers to attend school and have face to face classes. Also, during a new fall term and beyond, there will be hesitation among parents and students to attend school in person and online. As a result, if we cannot engage our students and parents,participation rates of students maybe much lower than a traditional term.

What must be taken into consideration is to ensure students with special needs can receive their specialized instruction online as well as in-person (Rice & Dykman, 2018). Finally, policymakers, educational leaders, and teachers must assess and evaluate how schools will navigate the next 12 to 18 months and beyond. There are a number of priorities they need to assess, which includes instituting social distancing protocols, hyper hygienic standards, staggered schedules, and online and blended learning models.

Furthermore, schools and districts need to set themselves up for 'continued learning' as a collection of ideas percolates online. District leaders, school administrators, and teachers need to be equipped with how to access this information to continue the professional learning process. All are critical in developing any plan to reopen in the fall safely and to provide quality instruction to their students.

How to Use this Book

The goal is for this to be a practical experience for you. By reading and taking the ideas presented in this book, you can further refine the ideas presented in this book and collaborate with stakeholders within your district and school to begin developing new plans for reopening schools. This book provides a number of recommendations to help prepare the reader for the fall and beyond.

1. **Read, Think, and Innovate:** From your own experiences of online learning that took place this past spring, your job is to read, think, and innovate through synthesizing this information with your experiences. Take ideas from this book and target how they can best apply to your current educational setting in your school and district.

2. **Collaborate with Others:** Collaboration will be one of the single-most important mechanisms we can use to develop

the best plans to reopen our schools. Each stakeholder in the education community needs to be consulted within this process as it is going to have high levels of complexity. By consulting others and collaborating using the ideas presented in this book, innovation and the application of ideas will occur.

3. **Use this Book as a Mechanism for Professional Learning:** Professional learning is necessary to ensure schools and districts are ready to reopen. All in an educational organization need to be trained in new protocols and instructional models to ensure on a systematic level, the reopening of schools can occur. By providing professional learning on the content outlined in this book, you will be prepared to provide content online, and face to face as well as be aware of the procedures that need to be in place for schools as an organization to reopen effectively.

Conclusion

Navigating the next 12 to 18 months and beyond look like having to implement some form of face to face instruction and online learning simultaneously. This will be a massive task that will take time to plan and implement. Secondary administrators and teachers must be pragmatic and collaborative to ensure it is done in a way so teachers and students can learn together in an environment that is safe. Currently, there is research and ideas available for educators to begin conceptualizing how to develop short term plans to initially reopen as well as long-term plans on how to navigate the future, which will be outlined throughout many of the chapters of this book (Ferdig & Kennedy, 2018). Learning is key to that process. Therefore, take in the information presented in this book, innovate, and then begin pragmatically planning to initially reopen with the ability to toggle back and forth between blended face to face and online learning and fully online instruction. Also, as you continue to navigate this book, keep an eye out on **www.matthewrhoads.com/blog** for more resources and information relating to the contents of this book to further expand your toolbox.

Ultimately, we can do this as an educational community. There is no doubt that K-12 education will overcome this challenge. Educators are some of the most passionate and hardworking individuals out there, which will go a long way in combating these challenges. Our efforts over the next 12 to 18 months will establish an educational environment that will be the mold that pulls communities together to rebuild once this pandemic has been overcome.

PART 1

Solidifying your Schools Edtech and Online Instructional Infrastructure

For our secondary schools to reopen and to ease back into face to face instruction, they must have a strong online instructional foundation in place. Right now, it is essential because there is now time to plan ahead, unlike in the spring of 2020. Schools are now in the position to refine their practices from the spring of 2020 to be successful in being able to reopen. This will allow schools to move back to solely online instruction if the number of COVID-19 cases increases to the point where attending school in any face to face capacity is deemed unsafe.

Having a robust edtech infrastructure is pertinent to being able to "toggle" back and forth between online instruction and blended learning instruction. What does this look like in practice? A robust edtech infrastructure involves educators from administrators to teachers to have the capacity to operate a learning management system, but also demonstrating the ability to disseminate between various edtech tools to supplement their instruction within the learning management system.

A learning management system is an online platform, for example, Google Classroom, Moodle, Canvas, Blackboard, Seesaw, and Schoology, where students interact with teacher-created content, assignments, and assessments for an online or blended learning course. To have successful online learning experiences, students must be able to use the learning management system as a foundational piece because the technological medium allows them to interact with the content, instructor, and other students (Hillman, Willis, and Gunawardena, 1994, p. 33). Furthermore, by integrating additional edtech tools and aligning instructional strategies that can be accomplished in both an online and face to face settings, it will prepare educators for navigating a toggled term as schools will begin reopening and easing into some form of blended face to face and online instruction.

To prepare educators for the possibility of a toggled term where online instruction will be the foundation of easing schools back to face to face instruction, part one will focus on providing educators a crash course in edtech and developing online learning platforms. Educators have been bombarded with many tools, and each successive chapter within part one addresses how to do this first by outlining a framework of how to select various edtech tools.

Chapter 1 provides a step by step process of how secondary educators can select edtech tools to facilitate their online instruction. Then, Chapter 2 will consist of a discussion on relevant edtech tools and applications that will be provided to review. After learning how to narrow down your edtech tools and evaluating a comprehensive list of what's available, Chapter 3 will outline the steps to build an online classroom that can also be used for blended learning settings. Lastly, Chapter 4 will integrate how lesson plans and instructional strategies can be synthesized together with edtech for online learning and blended learning classrooms.

CHAPTER 1

Selecting Edtech Tools for your Online and Blended Learning Classroom

When schools initially transitioned to distance learning, secondary educators were bombarded by a multitude of edtech tools to utilize for online classrooms. At times, it was overwhelming as many of us were scrambling to build an infrastructure for our online classes. Therefore, as we continue to think about building and refining our online classrooms, we wanted to describe the decision-making process for selecting edtech tools for your future online and blended learning classes. The goal of this chapter is to outline the **five steps** in selecting the best edtech tools for the online and blended learning classroom you are building and refining as we move towards reopening schools this fall.

Step 1: Think Less is More

To have a successful online classroom infrastructure, teachers need to be explicit in what they want students to do and have the mindset that less is more (Archer & Hughes, 2011). This is no different for an online or blended learning classroom. Teachers do not need more than four to five edtech tools to be successful because there are many instructional pathways teachers can take.

In order to employ the mindset of 'less is more,' there are four edtech components that create a foundation for a successful online and blended learning classroom: a learning management system, content creation edtech tools, a virtual online meeting tool, and student engagement edtech tools. First, you will need a learning management system to host your online and blended learning classroom (i.e., Google Classroom, Canvas, Schoology, Blackboard, Seesaw, etc.). Second, you will need Microsoft Office 365 or Google Apps to create content (i.e., Docs, Slideshows, PDF drawings, Data Spreadsheets, and Assessments). Third, you will need an online virtual meeting tool to host online synchronous learning sessions (i.e., Google Meet, Microsoft Teams, Zoom [if approved by your district], YoTeach!, etc.). Fourth, you will need one or two student engagement tools to make their synchronous and asynchronous engaging where students are actively learning (i.e., PearDeck, Flipgrid, Hyperdocs, Quizzizz, Classhooks, Poll Everywhere, Social Media interaction, etc.). As illustrated in Figure 1.1, once teachers have a learning management system, a platform to create digital content for students, and student engagement tools in place, teachers will have a robust edtech toolbox to develop an infrastructure to implement successful online and blended learning classrooms.

Learning Management Systems and Edtech Tools (i.e., Google Classroom, Canvas, Blackboard, Moodle, Powerschool, Schoology, Seesaw)		
Content Creation	**Virtual Synchronous Class Sessions**	**Student Engagement**
Microsoft Office 365 Google Apps	Google Meet Microsoft Teams Zoom AdobeConnect YoTeach!	PearDeck Flipgrid Hyperdocs Quizzizz Kahoot! Classhooks Poll Everywhere Social media platforms Whiteboard Fox

Figure 1.1. Mainstream Learning Management Systems and Edtech Tools

Step 2: Focus on the Audience and Goals

Know Your Audience. Next, teachers must focus on their student audience, instructional goals, and abilities of their students. First, teachers need to address what content and grade level they are teaching. For example, if a teacher is in primary school or teaching mathematics at the secondary level, Seesaw may be the best learning management system to use. On Seesaw, students can interact with documents teachers publish in a multitude of different (i.e., photos, video, and drawing/text on the document) ways due to the student interaction capabilities embedded in the software. As a result, students can take a picture of their work from a scratch piece of paper, draw on the document digitally on the Seesaw platform, or print out the assignment and snap a picture of it. All of these are options for students to interact with content in a multitude of different ways, give students options and choices. Overall, teachers must focus on their audience as specific edtech tools may not be geared towards a particular subject or age group of students.

Instructional Goals. Teachers must also think about their goals. Say you are a social science teacher with one or two Advanced Placement classes. Utilizing Google Classroom and Google Apps through G-Suite may be the best bet as you can integrate videos, links, documents, and more within slideshows or post within shared documents so students can interact with it an intuitive fashion.

Assessing Student Abilities. Teachers must also evaluate the ability and skill level of their students as well as assess how they can implement various accommodations and language supports for students enrolled in Special Education and English Language Learners. Assessment will give teachers data they can analyze to determine where their students are at in their academic abilities, which then can be used to develop curriculum. Additionally, assessment is used throughout the course of the year to monitor and adjust instruction and curriculum to meet students where they currently are at in their learning.

Assessing students with disabilities or English Language Learners can be difficult because each assessment tool must have accommodations in mind so students can be assessed equitably. Specific accommodations like highlighting key text, speech to text options, and read-aloud text functionalities are generally embedded in certain edtech tools (i.e., G-Suite), but not all. As a result, teachers must do their homework as to what accommodations can be best brought forth in the edtech tools they choose to assess their students with for their class.

By continually assessing students, it will allow teachers to know their students and meet them where they are at academically. Also, teachers will have the data to monitor and adjust their instruction to determine what steps need to be implemented on how to close achievement gaps in relation to their entire class as well as for individual students.

Step 3: Assess the Face to Face Class & Edtech Tools you Already Know

Before having to transition online, teachers need to assess how their face to face class functioned daily. For teachers at the primary level, did they utilize rotating stations on a daily or weekly basis? For teachers at the secondary level, how much direct instruction versus student collaboration and project-based learning strategies did they employ? These are essential questions to ask yourself.

Teachers should think about the edtech tools they are already using in their class. For many classes out there, several edtech tools are being used, whether it is tutorials on iPads, Google Classroom, Pear Deck for student engagement, or many more. For example, in my 9th-grade math class, each co-teacher utilized a gradual release of student responsibility through guided practice and then through collaborative/independent practice throughout our lessons (Pearson & Gallagher, 1984). We also used edtech tools such as Google Classroom, Docs, Forms, Draw, and Slides to build both online and offline functionalities to produce content and for our students to create student work products. As a result, we can develop an online class that fits this model as we can produce or find videos of math instruction that are embedded in instructional slides to lead our students through guided practice. Then, we can set up independent and collaborative student assignments through a learning management system, whereby we chose Seesaw instead of Google Classroom as it's much easier for students to interact with mathematics online versus face to face instruction. In terms of assessment, we utilized Google Forms and Quizizz for formative and summative assessments for their face to face classroom, which can also be used primarily for an online classroom and for blended learning educational settings. Through navigating through this step, we want you to realize much of what you may be already doing can be developed for online purposes with a few tweaks and one or two more edtech tools.

Step 4: Synchronous vs. Asynchronous Sessions

As an online instructor, secondary teachers need to determine how much time they want to dedicate to synchronous versus asynchronous sessions, which can then be integrated into a blended learning environment once schools begin reopening. Synchronous sessions involve having a live online class tutorial or lecture where the instructor meets with the entire class online at a given time. Asynchronous relates to having the content already built for students in a sequential manner in which they interact with the prebuilt content over the course of a given week or unit (Lowes & Kinghorn, 2015). Generally speaking, you want to avoid having more than two full synchronous sessions per week based on current online teaching best practices. Synchronous sessions are best suited to having online or in-person lessons (when it's a blended learning model) where active participation takes place. These live online or in-person class sessions can take place one to two times per week, where the entire class or groups of students can interact with their teacher. During these sessions, teachers can review the weekly content, provide instruction regarding assignments and tasks, have online class discussions and opportunities for student collaboration, provide opportunities for community building, and devote time to review general housekeeping questions regarding the course. However, we must keep in mind each school district and may have different philosophies' s/directives regarding synchronous and asynchronous instruction for online instruction and the blended learning environment. Right now, based on your district's privacy agreements, synchronous sessions are typically on an edtech tool like Google Meet, Microsoft Teams, or Zoom [Zoom Premium is HIPPA approved].

Step 5: Reflect and Revise One Week at a Time

Transitioning and teaching online in a full-time capacity may be perceived as adding several new job descriptions for many teachers. Teachers can take this opportunity as a time to learn and build their technical repertoire and instructional tool kit. Ultimately, teachers are going to have bumps in the road as well as triumphs; especially, if they are utilizing a new set of edtech tools. Teachers need to be sure to take their time in this reflection process as it takes practice. Additionally, it will take time for students to get used to the edtech tools you selected for your online and blended learning classroom. Ultimately, some days may be harder than others, so give yourself some time to process.

Selecting Edtech Tools – A Step by Step Process

As we go through each of the steps covered in this chapter, there are many different pathways teachers can take in selecting edtech tools for their online or blended learning classrooms. Figure 1.2 illustrates the thought processes of a primary and secondary teacher when selecting edtech tools for their classroom instruction and students. All educators, regardless of whether you are a teacher or school administrator, put yourself in their shoes as you review each of the steps outlined in this chapter. Then, select your edtech tools using these five steps for your own classroom, school, or district. Overall, these steps can be used throughout the entire school year to select your edtech tools, not just at the beginning of the school year. It is a continuous process that will need to be monitored and adjusted. Over time, more edtech tools may be implemented based on student needs and the type of instruction that is delivered to students. Or, for the same reasons, fewer edtech tools may be needed.

Selecting Edtech Tools		
Steps	**Primary**	**Secondary**
Step 1: Think Less is More	**Tools to Choose From: Choose 4** Seesaw, Google Classroom, Canvas, Schoology, Canvas, Flipgrid, Freckle, Achieve 3000, MobyMax, Loom, Pear Deck, Lexia, Screencastify, Microsoft Teams, Zoom, Google Meet	**Tools to Choose From: Choose 4** Seesaw, Google Classroom, Canvas, Schoology, Canvas, G-Suite, Microsoft 365, Flipgrid, Freckle, Achieve 3000, Desmos, Loom, Pear Deck, Screencastify, Khan Academy, Microsoft Teams, Zoom, Google Meet
Step 2: Focus on the Audience and Goals	**Audience:** 1st Grade, 22 General Education Students, 3 Special Education Students, and 2 English Language Learners. **Goals:** Engagement, Reading Comprehension, Number Sense	**Audience:** 10th Grade, World History, 35 General Education Students, 5 Special Education Students, and 2 English Language Learners. **Goals:** Student Choice, Writing Thesis Statements, Embedding Textual Evidences, and Analyzing Evidence
Step 3: Assess your Face to Face Class & Edtech Tools you Already Know	**Face to Face (before shutdown):** We utilized Seesaw for turning in some of our work. I also used centers as a way for students to create student work. Half of all student work was done on paper. **Tools I Know:** Seesaw, G-Suite, Achieve 3000, Microsoft Teams, and MobyMax	**Face to Face (before shutdown):** Each week, my class had one weekly lecture, one homework packet relating the chapter, and a team collaboration project. We used Google Classroom to turn in major assignments. **Tools I Know:** Google Classroom, G-Suite, and Khan Academy

Step 4: Synchronous vs. Asynchronous Sessions	**Synchronous:** Heterogenous ELA and Math Groups (30 minutes each per subject, 1 hour total per day); 4 days a week Monday-Thursday; One on One Tutorials on Fridays. **Asynchronous:** 3 hours per day of ELA and Math activities	**Synchronous:** Two Full Online Class Sessions a Week (2 hours); Office Hours Monday – Friday 1:00 – 3:00 pm. **Asynchronous:** 1 hour of asynchronous work per day (5 hours a week).
Initial Tools Selected (Choose 4)	Seesaw, Microsoft Teams, Achieve 3000, and G-Suite	Google Classroom, G-Suite, Google Meet, and Khan Academy
Step 5: Reflect and Revise One Week at a Time	**How did it go?** Seesaw was able to be the platform I posted my reading and math activities on for the week. Students turned in their work without issue, and I was able to give feedback. I used G-Suite to create my assignments. I enjoyed Achieve 3000, but I also need a math edtech tool that I can use for my students for further practice and differentiating the instruction for all of the learners I have in my class.	**How did it go?** Google Classroom and Google Meet went well. I used our synchronous time to work in breakout rooms on a collaborative project on analyzing evidence from a primary source we are working on this week. Khan Academy was used for a lecture supplement. Still, I am unsure if I need it moving forward because we are focusing more on skills than content knowledge on historical events.
Long Term Tools (Choose 3, 4 or 5)	Seesaw, G-Suite, Microsoft Teams, Achieve 3000, and MobyMax	Google Classroom, G-Suite, and Google Meet

Figure 1.2. Selecting your Edtech Tools

Conclusion

Before moving on, be sure to reflect your thoughts towards the online class you have built using the edtech tools you have selected. As districts and schools plan to reopen to some form of face to face instruction, online classrooms will be integrated into a blended learning educational setting. Therefore, teachers need to think about the following as they continue refining their practice as online instructors. The latter will eventually be easing synchronous class sessions into face to face instruction as blended learning models become more prevalent as schools begin reopening. First, evaluate whether problems arose during the weeks and months when you began implementing your online class. Second, assess whether your students were engaged and understood the directions. Lastly, determine if there was a digital divide in your class, and time may be needed to be given to teaching your students further how to use the edtech tools you have decided to utilize to build your online class. Also, during this process, reflect whether you have selected the sufficient edtech tools for your class. If something was not working regarding the edtech tools you selected, go back to the drawing board and see how you can fix the problems you were having. Or, you may have to select a new edtech tool to fix the problem. Thus, revise your online classroom platform, as needed, as you continue to learn how to use edtech tools as this is a continuous process as more capacity for edtech and online learning is developed.

CHAPTER 2

Edtech Tools to Get You Started with Your Online and Blended Teaching! Start Now!

As classrooms in schools moved online during the spring of 2020, there were a plethora of edtech tools available to use. After having a good idea of how to select edtech tools, we must now understand which edtech tools can apply to your classroom setting. It is vital to continue learning about edtech tools and their various applications for online and blended learning classrooms as many of the instructional models for the 2020-2021 school year and beyond will need edtech tools to make them happen. Within this chapter, there is a comprehensive list of mainstream edtech tools utilized by expert teachers in the field of education technology that has been used often in both online and face to face secondary classrooms. Ultimately, this means that the edtech tools can also be employed in a blended learning environment when schools initially reopen for the fall 2020 semester and beyond. Within this list, each edtech tool is defined, and its uses and applications for online and face to face classrooms are provided. Additionally, within each description of the edtech tool, links are provided to a resource that further discusses each edtech tool more in-depth than what has been discussed on this list.

To be most effective with your time, take what you have learned from Chapter 1 on selecting edtech tools for your classroom while reviewing each edtech tool and its applications for secondary instruction. To be successful in using edtech, knowledge about every tool is not what makes for successful instruction. Ultimately, it is a three-step process that requires three elements in alignment for secondary teachers to be successful in utilizing edtech. First, by having an understanding of the edtech tools capabilities and synthesizing it with best practice instructional strategies is what makes teachers successful in utilizing edtech. Second, as you evaluate this list, try to find at least **three** edtech tools you would like to check out and integrate into your lessons beyond what you are currently using now. Third, do not go overboard. Start simply and then expand your edtech toolbox over time. Remember, each of these tools has many uses, which means there is a wide range of instructional strategies that can be used in an online and blended learning classroom setting.

Edtech Tool Application and Uses

Google Classroom: Google Classroom is a mainstream online learning management system (U.S. Department of Education, 2017). This learning management system allows teachers to post and grade assignments, organize student work into tabs/modules,Google Meet is integrated for synchronous live classes, embedded online grade book, student/family communication tool, multiple-choice assessments can be posted and graded, writing rubrics can be developed on the platform, and for materials and videos can be linked to assignments.

Google Forms: Google Forms can be utilized to develop formative and summative assessments, climate surveys (i.e., student, parent, teachers, etc.), and student metacognition (i.e., self-assessment) surveys. There is a multitude of different question types that range from multiple-choice, Likert scale, to free-response that Google Forms can utilize. Images and videos can also be attached to each question or various areas of the survey or assessment. Google Forms can be posted on any learning management system as it only needs student email addresses to track the data entered on the survey or teacher-created assessment.

Google Drive: Online data storage cloud that allows you to save G-Suite files, videos, images, PDFs, and more as well as organize files into various folders. Files can be uploaded and downloaded from Google Drive. Additionally, Google Drive can be integrated with your Google Classroom or any other learning management software. Be aware of modifying your sharing settings when this occurs, as you will want to determine who has access to the online folders.

Google Slides: Google Slides are the PowerPoint of G-Suite. It allows users to build slideshows with information and resources embedded within them. Teachers can use Google Slides for oral/visual presentations, poster boards, online gallery walk, a-z vocabulary, and can be used to create individual and collaborative projects. Google Slides can be posted on Google Classroom, Canvas, Blackboard, and Schoology for students to either view or interact with directly for an individual or collaborative assignment.

Google Docs: Google Docs is the Word Document tool found in G-Suite. For classroom or online use, Docs can be used to create digital reading passages where students can read/annotate, graphic organizers, essays, poems, and short works. Google Docs can be collaborative, where multiple students can work on it at once by modifying the sharing options of the document. Also, Google Docs can be commented on by different users who do not have privileges to edit the document, which can be used for editing/revising pieces of writing. Teachers can use Google Docs as the primary EdTech Tool for reading/writing assignments that can be added to either Google Classroom or any other online learning management system (i.e., Seesaw, Canvas, Blackboard, and Schoology).

Google Draw: Google Draw allows users to develop pictures and graphics that can be placed on Google Docs, Slides, Sites, etc. Teachers can utilize Google Draw to have students develop graphic organizers, digital poster boards, infographics, and more. Google Draw can be posted on any learning management system.

Google Sheets: Google Sheets is the Excel of G-Suite. Data can be recorded in an organized manner (this includes both text and numeric data). Teachers can use Google Sheets in Math and Science classes to help students learn how to analyze data, develop graphs, and conduct statistical analysis.

Google Sites: Google Sites is a platform where users can build an entire functioning website. It provides a platform for users to place text, audio, video, graphics, and more. Teachers can use Google Sites as a platform for students to obtain resources/assignments, an assignment where students and teachers can develop their own website/blog, and much more.

Pear Deck: Pear Deck is an add-on to Google Slides, which allows for students to participate during a Google Slides presentation actively (Pear Deck, 2020). Multiple choice, free response, word webs/mind maps, formative assessment, multiple-choice questions, and more can be used to facilitate active student participation. Further, Pear Deck allows the teacher to see overall student participation and responses to make data-driven decisions regarding the focus of the presentation/content based on student responses.

Flipgrid: Flipgrid is a student video/audio recording software that allows a teacher to pose a question online that students must respond to via audio and video (Flipgrid, 2020). Students can see the question presented by the teacher in addition to other student responses. Assessment rubrics can be built in Flipgrid to assess student responses.

Flipgrid can also be used for an in-class and online instructional setting.

Screencast-o-Matic, Screencastify, and Loom: Screencasting is the ability to record the video and audio of a user's computer screen and/or a video of themselves (Loom, 2020; Screencastify, 2020; Screencast-o-Matic, 2020). By capturing a computer's video and audio, viewers can watch the video as a tutorial to help them learn the directions of how to do something. Teachers can utilize screencasts as a way to frontload content, model instruction, formative/summative assessment, and provide additional resources to their students.

Kahoot, Quizzizz, and GoFormative: Kahoot, Quizizz, and Formative are three online formative and summative assessment tools (Jones, 2020; Kahoot, 2020; Quizzizz, 2020). Teachers have the ability to create a wide range of questions students can answer via a Chromebook or Smartphone. Data from student answers are given to teachers thereafter to determine how students did on the assessment. Kahoot and Quizizz can be linked to any online learning management system.

Khan Academy: Khan Academy is a free online class resource and tutorial where students can watch videos and complete practice problems on major subjects ranging from World History, Algebra 2, Biology, and ACT/SAT prep (Khan Academy, 2020). Teachers can use Khan Academy as an additional enrichment tool or even as a differentiation tool for students who may need additional reinforcement of concepts covered in class. Khan Academy can be linked to any online learning management system.

EdPuzzle: Edpuzzle is a free online resource where teachers can utilize one of its many videos and assess student comprehension of the content being presented in the video (Edpuzzle, 2020). Teachers can use Edpuzzle as a tutorial to reinforce a concept, frontloading information, and as an option to assess student progress. Edpuzzle can be easily integrated into several Learning Management Systems, including Google Classroom.

Padlet: Padlet allows users to build online poster boards, documents, and webpages. It can also allow users to work together on projects collaboratively (Padlet, 2020). Teachers can use Padlet for students to create infographics, websites, and graphics relating to the content being discussed in class. Padlet can be linked to any online learning management system.

Readtheory: Readtheory is a free online reading comprehension practice tool for students of all grade levels and reading levels (Readtheory, 2020). Students initially take a pretest, and then Readtheory adapts its passages and questions to their Lexile level from their score on the pretest. From there, the passages and questions increase in their difficulty as students' progress in their reading ability. On the teacher interface, teachers can see student progress overtime by seeing their current Lexile level, Lexile growth, and the types of questions students do well on versus questions students need improvement in to improve their scores.

Common Lit: CommonLit is a free online reading passage generator tool for students grades 3-12 to interact with online reading passages to help improve students improve their literacy skills (CommonLit, 2020). Students receive a passage where they can read/annotate. Once they are done, they must answer a variety of question types ranging from multiple choice to short answer; many of which are CAASPP like. Teachers can set the passage provided to students with the content they are learning in their class. Also, teachers can see student growth over time in terms of their reading ability. Lastly, CommonLit can be linked to any learning management system.

YoTeach!: YoTeach! is an online collaborative educational backchannel chatroom that can be developed for your class (YoTeach!, 2020). Once the room is developed, students will always have access to the room through a password created. Within the chatroom, it functions as a place where content can be presented visually and through audio/video. Teachers can use this tool to deliver content, use it as a means to have active student participation, and it can be utilized for students to work together collaboratively in class and outside of class.

b.Socrative: b.socrative is an online formative and summative assessment tool students (b.Socrative, 2020). Teachers can develop their own assessments or choose from many different types of prebuilt assessments in all subject areas to give to their students. Students can complete the assessment on a computer or mobile phone. b.socrative provides real-time data to determine where your students are at on the content seamlessly and efficiently. Teachers can export the data onto an Excel spreadsheet to be placed in their grade book.

Wiki's: Wiki's are an online information resource that students can develop individually or collaboratively on a given topic (Wikipedia, 2020). We all know what Wikipedia is - Wiki's are very familiar in terms of their format and use. Teachers can develop Wiki's for their class; students can develop Wikis for individual and collaborative projects. Wiki's can be linked in any online learning management system.

GroupMaker: Groupmaker is a free online program that allows teachers to randomize groups on the fly in their classes as well as randomize cold calling on students in a class.

WhiteBoard Fox: White Board Fox is an online collaborative whiteboard where students can enter, and teachers/students can present content written onto an interactive whiteboard (Whiteboard Fox,

2020). Teachers can use this tool for active participation and groups/ class collaboration. The link to the Whiteboard can be posted on any learning management system.

Geoguessr: Geoguessr is an online context clue guessing game where students are directed to locate a location somewhere in the world (Geoguessr, 2020). It utilizes Google Earth and Street to place the user on a random street somewhere in the world. The student must use context clues such as language, the side of the streetcars are going, the landscape, and more to guess where in the world, the street view is located. Geoguessr can be linked to any learning management system.

Types of Edtech Tools

Beyond the edtech tools discussed above, there are many more that are available. Figure 2.1 illustrates the edtech tools described above, as well as several others that have been added. Many of the edtech tools provided below are within the mainstream of edtech tools readily available to educators to use at the secondary level for their blended learning or online classroom (note Figure 2.1 does not include them all). Now, take a moment and write down which edtech tools you already know about and know how to use and apply to your classroom. Then, in the other column, write down which tools you have not heard about so far. Finally, in the final column, write down the tools you know about but do not know how to use and apply it to your classroom. Once you are done with creating three separate lists, be ready to use this list by reviewing Chapter 2 once again by selecting your edtech tools. Then, when moving forward to Chapter 3, there will be an opportunity to integrate the selected edtech tools into your online and blended learning classroom platform.

Types of Edtech Tools – Mainstream Tools for K-12 Education Available for Secondary Educators		
Assessment • Google Forms • Formative • EdPuzzle • b.socrativ • Kahoot • Quizizz • Common Lit	**Active Engagement** • Pear Deck • Geoguesser • Poll Everywhere • YoTeach! • Flipgrid	**Student Work Creation** • Google G-Suite (i.e., Docs, Slides, Sheets, Sites, Drive, and Draw) • Microsoft 365 • Padlet • Canva • Storyboardthat • Wiki's
Adaptive Edtech • Achieve 3000 • Read 180 • MobyMax • Freckle • Readtheory • Lexia • Dreambox • iReady • Reflex	**Modeling Instruction** • Screencastify • Loom • Screencast-O-Matic • Whiteboard Fox	**Learning Management Systems** • Google Classroom • Seesaw • Powerschool • Canvas • Blackboard • Schoology
Synchronous Session Platform • Google Meet • Microsoft Teams • Adobe Connect • Zoom	**Misc** • GroupMaker • Rewordify • Word Cloud Generator • Nod	**Tutorial** • Khan Academy • Desmos

Figure 2.1. Mainstream Edtech Tools Available for Secondary Educators

Conclusion

The list of edtech tools provided in this chapter is just a start of the possibilities out there with some of the available free mainstream edtech tools. Ultimately, there are endless options educators can choose from for their online and blended learning classrooms. However, more important than the tools themselves is to be sure to select the proper edtech tool for the students you serve in your classroom or school. On top of this is the ability to interconnect the edtech tools you select to instructional strategies that can be used to teach your students the content and skills your class or grade level is geared towards doing.

Now, after seeing how we can select edtech tools as well as see a glimpse at the possibilities that are out there to incorporate the tools into an online or blended learning classroom, it's time to learn how to build and refine your classrooms for the fall semester. Building an online classroom is key to developing a platform, your students can access content, whether it is an online or blended learning instructional setting. Additionally, by having an online classroom, regardless of whether schools open with face to face instruction, it allows for students in a digitally connected world to always access their learning 24/7.

CHAPTER 3

Steps to Building Your Online Classroom for Secondary Educators

Building an online classroom in a matter of days during the spring of 2020 was daunting. Many educators described the process as schools recreating the wheel when this occurred. Consequently, building an online platform when having to move back and forth from a face to face learning experience to an online one will be one of the remedies for this challenge. With careful thought and planning, moving to a class online at a moment's notice does not have to be as tumultuous as it sounds because having an online infrastructure in place will ensure moving back and forth is swift and painless. Thus, we want to provide a step by step process to successfully plan for a transition to a blended learning classroom as well as to maintain an online classroom in the event having to toggle between face to face and online education settings. As a result, the goal here is to take secondary educators through the thought process of how this can be done. A variety of steps will be broken down throughout to help teachers to create a best practice online classroom that can also be utilized in a blended learning format once schools begin initially reopening to some form of face to face instruction.

Provided in this chapter are **eight steps** that will aid teachers in their thinking, planning, and refining their future online classroom. There may be steps that could beharder than others as well as steps that require a 'wait and see' approach due to awaiting directives from districts and schools regarding how conceptually online instruction and blended learning will look like for teachers in the fall and beyond. This is okay because some of the significant legwork and planning can take place as information comes out from our district offices as we plan to launch our online and blended learning classrooms in addition to refining the plans over time as we navigate the toggled term. During this time, we encourage teachers to think of new ways of how they can reinvent their classrooms because educational settings will look vastly different next semester. It is time to innovate and experiment. By focusing on the following eight steps, let the experimentation and innovation begin.

Step 1: Review your District's Directive/Vision of Online Learning and Blended Learning

Understanding what the expectations are regarding online and blended learning is critical. At one end of the spectrum, an online class can be completely asynchronous, which means its module is driven whereby a student goes at their own pace to learn the content provided by the teacher without much direct communication from the teacher. Or, in contrast, online classes can be more synchronous instruction is live by a teacher going through the content, which means more time will be dedicated to actual 'class time.' This can also manifest itself when schools begin initially reopening and when some form of face to face instruction begins taking place in the form of a blended learning model. So far, across the U.S., we have seen K-12 provide a mix of synchronous and asynchronous instruction expectations being provided by districts. One of the best practice models used to provide secondary online instruction in the spring of 2020 was scheduled one or two hours a week per class of synchronous instruction, along with dedicated office hours that are optional for students (Casey, 2020).

Then, outside of the synchronous instruction and office hours, the remainder of the class can be built in an asynchronous fashion where students can work at their own pace throughout the week on the content created by their teacher. Once assignments or tasks have been completed by students, they can receive feedback from their teacher on a daily or weekly basis, depending on workflow expectations for the class.

Above all, read the expectations and ask questions, if needed, once districts and schools begin providing directives towards what is expected in the fall. At this point, there will be a little rigidity. Still, since it is a new territory for districts and schools, there will be flexibility to experiment and learn, which ultimately will be the best for students and teachers alike. Thus, be sure to consult your districts and stay proactive. As more information comes out, address it and move it into your thinking and development processes for your online and blended learning classroom.

Step 2: Get familiar with the District Supported Learning Management System and Edtech Tools

Learning management systems are a centralized online infrastructure in which all content is created and posted by a teacher and then interacted with by both students and the teacher. Google Classroom, Blackboard, Canvas, Schoology, Moodle, Powerschool, and Seesaw are all popular learning management systems being used in K-12 schools across the country. Many learning management systems have a learning curve, but that does not mean they are not intuitive to learn. To be successful with learning management systems is to focus on the following steps to get the most out of the learning management system you are working with to benefit your students and your workflow:

- Getting students to join your classroom.

- Interconnecting teacher and student created content (i.e., Google Apps, Microsoft 365) as they are used to create content, tasks, and assignments.

- How to post assignments and ensure students have access to all of their materials.

- How to grade student work and then transfer the assessed work to the grade book.

- Student communication.

- Content/assignment organization to create a user-friendly interface for your students.

- Integrating other edtech tools into the learning management classroom.

To begin, for Google Classroom, knowledge of Google Apps within G-Suite and how they interact amongst each is extremely important. If you know the basics of Docs, Slides, Draw, and Sheets, you should not have any problems creating content, tasks, or assignments. It does not have to be overly sophisticated to be effective content for your students to interact with through the learning management system. Then, once you have an idea of how to create content, Google Classroom allows you to post assignments and material under "classwork," which allows students to get their own copy of the assignment or material to interact with it. After creating an assignment, you will be notified when a student turns in work. Teachers can then grade the assignment and leave comments within the grading interface. However, at first, your grade book in your student information system is likely not interconnected. As a result, you will have to transfer the grades over from Google Classroom (some districts do have the ability to transfer Google Classrooms grade book to the student information systems grade book). Student communication is relatively intuitive as email addresses of all of your students are provided once they join your classroom (even parents can be invited to auditing a class). Lastly and most importantly, Google Classroom allows you to organize it by providing tabs in which assignments and content material can be organized underneath. Ultimately, if students know where the assignments and content are, it will make it much easier for them to navigate the interface.

Step 3: Determine how your Online Classroom will Function

This statement is ambiguous for a reason because all classes are different depending on their content, student population, grade level, and teacher. For example, in our 9th-grade math class that transitioned online demonstrates how the very structure of the class shifted to meet the needs of our students when the educational setting switched. In the face to face version of the class, we provided a gradual release model of instruction where we modeled how to complete math problems in a variety of different ways. Then, we allowed students to grapple with the content during either independent practice or student collaboration. Once we were able to monitor how the class was doing with the content, we made either individual adjustments or stopped the entire class to provide modeling further to help clarify with our students or address any conclusion. Formative assessment was conducted twice a week, typically for us to see how our students were doing on content (generally in the middle and at the end of the week). This allowed us time to monitor and adjust instruction and help individual students with the content.

Now, when planning, developing, and refining our online class as the transition occurred to online distance learning, we decided to provide online math videos (i.e., YouTube and Khan Academy) and screencasts for the asynchronous portion of the class. By doing this for our students, they could view the math instruction as many times as they needed at their own pace. What was successful was being able to frontload the content asynchronously, which allowed our students to practice the material independently. Then, using formative assessment more directly, weposted at least two formative assessments weekly in the form of interactive slides through Pear Deck and Google Forms. Through formative assessment, it allowed us to monitor individual and whole-class progress on the content. Summative assessments were posted intermittently throughout the month using Quizizz, Formative, and Google Forms. Office hours, in addition to synchronous instruction time, was used to attend to any student confusion or provide additional support. We addressed any discrepancies or questions on the content by modeling practice problems, assessing our students on the spot by providing feedback with interactive slides, and more resources to our students to help seek to address discrepancies in their learning. Regardless of content and grade level, this model can provide a framework of how you can develop and refine your online classroom.

Ultimately, having an online classroom is not entirely different than a face to face classroom. What it comes down to is the delivery of instruction. As a result, each class format is somewhat similar in structure but delivered differently. Through this process of continued transition and refinement, classrooms can be transformed in a similar manner to be interchangeable with online or blended learning as the fundamental structure of the classes may not be entirely changing when a triggered switch educational settings occur, which is a win for teachers and students adjusting to online and blended learning classrooms.

Step 4: Synchronous vs. Asynchronous Time

What this comes down to is how much time is being spent delivering content and instruction live versus creating content for your students to work on independently at their own pace. Depending on the type of teacher you are, you are likely better in creating synchronous or asynchronous content more than the other. Right now, as you get started with developing your online and blended learning classroom, you will likely have to get better with creating content using a multitude of different edtech tools to supplement the learning management system being utilized. For additional edtech tools for synchronous or asynchronous instruction, the learning curve here is equally as much because it depends on how they are utilized for each type of instructional delivery. Be sure to think about how and why you are using a specific edtech tool to augment your instruction. As discussed in Chapter 2, there is not a need to overdo the number of edtech tools that are used.

The best practice for synchronous learning sessions is that they only take place once or twice a week for whole-class settings (Hirumi, 2014). Therefore, where most of the student learning will take place is during asynchronous instruction, which is then supplemented by synchronous class sessions. In the fall, the online synchronous class sessions can be replaced with face to face class sessions when blended learning models are implemented with staggered schedules and social distancing protocols. As a result, more time may be dedicated to synchronous instruction as the easing of social distancing occurs over time. However, regardless of whether the synchronous class sessions are online or face to face, asynchronous instruction will require much more time on the student's behalf.

How does this instructional delivery look like throughout the week? Figure 3.1 provides two types of online class weekly schedules outlining days dedicated to synchronous vs. asynchronous instruction secondary schools can utilize for online or blended learning models. As you can see, each schedule dedicates the same number of synchronous minutes but allocated throughout the week differently. These types of schedules will translate to fall because they provide for days that were once dedicated to online synchronous instruction can be transformed into opportunities for in-person face to face synchronous instruction.

Monday	Tuesday	Wednesday	Thursday	Friday
Asynchronous	Asynchronous Office Hours Available	Synchronous Full Class (1-1 hour and half)	Asynchronous	Asynchronous Office Hours Available
Synchronous - Full Class (30 minutes to an hour)	Asynchronous	Asynchronous Synchronous Office Hours Available	Asynchronous	Synchronous - Full Class (30 minutes to an hour)

Figure 3.1. Synchronous and Asynchronous Weekly Instructional Calendars

Overall, there is a multitude of different options relating to determining your weekly online or blended learning schedule. Our hope is your district and school will give you some latitude in how much time you can dedicate to synchronous vs. asynchronous online instructional time. Then, when schools begin to reopen, more definitive times will be given for face to face instruction as staggered schedules are developed for one or more days per week.

Step 5: Build content inside your Google Drive with G-Suite Applications and Organize it into Weekly Folders

Building content can take time, but if you build an organizational structure within the content creating edtech tools you have at your disposal, it can be done efficiently and effectively. Generally speaking, it will take the most time to build your organizational system and the initial content for your class. After that, unless a complete redesign of the online classroom is needed, refining the classroom does not take nearly as long. An effective online classroom with synchronous elements will not take much to be integrated into a weekly face to face class. Now, for organizing the files for your online classroom, we are going to be using G-Suite as the example for this step because many school districts throughout the U.S. are using Google Classroom as their learning management system. Be sure to note that a similar organization method can be used on Microsoft 365. In Figure 3.2, take a look at the number of folders you will need to build within your Google Drive to create an infrastructure that is needed to develop an online classroom. Each folder contains major components of what is needed to develop a functioning online classroom. Next, analyze the following steps that have been outlined for you to help build the backend infrastructure of an online classroom within the context of G-Suite.

Figure 3.2. Google Drive Folders for Google Classroom

1. **A Class Folder on Google Drive.** Within the class folder (as seen above), create several other folders that include: Week 1, Week 2, Week 3, etc., Assessments, and Resources.

2. **Create a Backwards Planner on a Google Doc and Place into Class Folder.** A backward planner allows you to build your weeks' worth of asynchronous and synchronous

content. Backward planners are organized by day, have an underlining standard (for the week), and have hyperlinks to the content/assignments you will be sharing with your students

3. **Create HyperDocs/Slides.** Within each "week" folder, you will need to create a Google Slides Hyperdoc, which is an informational slideshow that provides your student's links to content (videos, articles, infographics, images, quizzes, etc.) and activities they will interact with throughout the week.

4. **Organize Assignments into Weekly Folders.** Within each "week" folder, you will need to develop at least one to two assignments you will want to post on your learning management system. These assignments can be short at first. You will want to make sure you go with the approach LESS is MORE as you get started. Assignments can be created using Google Docs, Slides, Sheets, and Draw in G-Suite; all can be posted on Google Classroom.

5. **Assessments.** Create at least ONE formative assessment per week, which can be done using Google Forms. The assessment can be placed within your "assessments folder."

6. **Resources Folder & Syllabus.** Within the "resources" folder, you will place your digital syllabus. Also, you will put any necessary documents from the district or your school site that must be shared with families on your learning management system.

Each of these steps outlined above is critical in getting started using G-Suite. Being organized digitally is just as important as being organized with paper, and it makes a massive difference in terms of the workflow for teachers and students for online classrooms. As a result, this workflow organization helps teachers build an initial online infrastructure that they can then continually build and add onto overtime.

Step 6: Select other Edtech Tools to Integrate into your Learning Management System

Selecting other edtech tools to integrate into their learning management system is a crucial thought process, and decisions teachers will have to go through as they build their online and blended learning classrooms. Teachers need to be aware not to add many other edtech tools outside of the content creation applications (i.e., G-Suite, Microsoft 365) at first when building their learning management system infrastructure and teacher-created content. However, as time progresses, teachers will want to add one to five additional edtech tools to integrate into the learning management system to help with student engagement, assessment, and student collaboration. Take a moment while evaluating this step to reference back to Chapter 2 as it describes several popular edtech tools and applications that can be integrated into your learning management. Remember, less is more in an online classroom initially, notably, at the beginning of the semester. But, over time, add a few more edtech tools as the semester progresses (likely by Week 4 or 6).

When selecting these additional edtech tools to integrate into an online classroom, we want you to think about your audience, student population, grade level, content, instructional strategies utilized in the past for face to face classes, and edtech tools you are already familiar with. These are all essential variables to think about while making decisions regarding your practices as a teacher going into a new semester.

Step 7: Create a Syllabus and Send to Parents and Students that Includes the Instructional Model

Before launching your classroom, you will need to develop and add to your syllabus information about the online or blended learning model that will occur to illustrate to parents and students the new expectations. This is entirely new and uncharted waters. Parents and students will need to be informed as to what this will be like going forward in the fall. Included in your expectations within the syllabus for the fall semester, teachers should outline the following for parents and students:

- A weekly schedule and information about how the class will run.
- Grading policies.
- How to communicate with teachers online and face to face.
- Attendance (districts may have to provide this information; it will depend on the state).
- Explanations regarding asynchronous instruction and face to face and online synchronous instruction.
- Information on how to join the learning management system for students and parents.
- Any other information provided by the district or school parents should know about.

Ultimately, this list does not include any information your district may want you to add. Although an expansion to your syllabus is vital, to ensure parents and students receive the syllabus, send it in an email at least 3 to 5 days out of your online launch for the semester to prepare your students and parents with the new expectations. Then, place the syllabus online on the learning management system for the school year.

Step 8: Post the First Week's Content and Assignments and Hit the Ground Running

On the Sunday before your online or blended learning class is about to begin, post all of your first week's content and assignments on your learning management system. Have everything posted and ready to go, so once Monday morning begins, your students will have everything they need for week one of the semester. Additionally, before officially launching the class, give yourself some time to test what you have built by accessing the class via a "teacher made student" mode (which is making a student profile for your learning management system and logging in as a student) to ensure all of the content and assignments are accessible and working. By doing this, you are making sure all of the major bugs are worked out before your students arrive and join your learning management system. However, know that during the first few weeks, there will be hiccups, which is entirely normal. By being prepared, you will be able to fix them appropriately. Lastly, as a new model of learning begins this fall, everyone, including your students and parents, will give you grace as the fall semester begins.

Conclusion

The goal in Chapter 3 was to provide a step by step guide to secondary teachers and administrators to go through some of the initial steps in setting up an online classroom as their primary classroom platform for the fall semester and beyond to navigate the toggled term. This goes to say that in all likelihood, the online classroom at the secondary level will be the base of all instruction whether the semester begins in a blended learning or online classroom when schools open up once again. Thus, teachers and administrators need to give themselves time to work together to collaboratively complete this task as it will not be done effectively overnight. Overall, developing an effective online classroom is doable if you give yourself ample time and are strategic about developing your online classroom. Teachers, schools, and administrators can do this. Keep learning and practice! It can be done.

To continue facilitating the development of your online classroom, we recommend seeking out help and looking at articles and tutorials online to help you learn the edtech tools you may need to launch your online class successfully. Remember, as with anything new you are learning, it will take practice. Lastly, as further outlined later on in part three of this book, we recommend going on Twitter and exploring various hashtags to help with your professional development and to keep up with new developments in edtech, education, and instructional strategies. Overall, developing an effective online classroom is doable if you give yourself some time and are strategic about how you develop your online classroom. You can do this. Keep learning and practice as it will get more comfortable with repetition!

CHAPTER 4

Implementing Instructional Strategies and Lesson Plans with Edtech for your Online Classrooms

Building an effective online classroom platform using a learning management system and several additional edtech tools is the first step in creating a best practice online and blended learning classroom. What needs to be further addressed and discussed by the educational community is in implementing and aligning various research-based instructional strategies with the edtech that is being used in our online and blended learning classrooms. Within Chapter 4, our goal is to provide teachers and administrators with a series of instructional strategies that can be used in a face to face classroom in addition to an online classroom. Going beyond this, there will be a discussion of which edtech tools can facilitate the outlined instructional strategies.

While implementing various instructional strategies, we want to ensure our synchronous, and asynchronous lessons are composed of listening, speaking, writing, and student work creation components (National Center on Universal Design for Learning, 2010). By having online and blended learning lessons that are multimodality in their composition, they fulfill the elements of the Universal Design for Learning, which allow for a more customizable and personalized experience for a single student or a group of students (Keeler et al., 2007). This is important as we are trying to facilitate student learning for all students, which helps us differentiate and personalize instruction for students who may need additional support in their learning (Rose & Blomeyer, 2007).

Three main topics will be outlined in Chapter 4. First, a list of instructional strategies we use in face to face classrooms that can also be used online. Second, we will describe how they can be implemented in an online classroom. Lastly, we will be going to provide an example of a weekly online class lesson plan outline that employs a multimodality approach.

Instructional Strategies Linked with Edtech

Instruction within a classroom can take many shapes and forms. Targeting various instructional strategies to your students to learn content is key to helping your students build efficacy and demonstrate academic growth. All instructional strategies can be integrated and even enhanced with edtech. Thus, this discussion will focus on nine mainstream best practice instructional strategies that have been shown to increase student academic achievement utilized in tandem with a variety of edtech tools. Each instructional strategy outlined here can be used within a face to face class setting as well as an online classroom, which makes them essential to learn regardless of your present educational setting(s).

Direct Instruction and Modeling in Synchronous/ Asynchronous Sessions. As with any classroom, direct instruction is used to provide instructions as well as give students information directly step by step on the content or skills being taught (Synder et al., 2014). Within synchronous live sessions on Google Meet, Microsoft Teams, or Zoom, teachers can share their screen and present Google Slides, Slideshare, Padlet, or Microsoft Powerpoint to depict the information they are lecturing on to their students. During direct instruction, teachers can use modeling to show their entire class or specific students how to perform a specific task or problem by sharing their screen with students and go through it step by step. Within this modeling technique, teachers can scaffold the tasks for their students and build a progression of videos their students can view within a module or unit of study. One central point of emphasis, all synchronous live direct instruction should be recorded for later student review (when possible based on privacy recommendations provided by the district). Ultimately, this will provide your students with an opportunity to review the content at any time and at their own pace (Synder et al., 2014).

For asynchronous sessions, teachers can use Screencast-o-Matic, Loom, or Screencastify to record a lecture that allows them to present content. Additionally, within each of these screencasting tools, they provide editing software to edit the recorded lectures for uploading to YouTube, Google Drive, iCloud, or DropBox. Once the lectures have been posted online within the storage cloud, teachers can use hyperlinks to place the links on a HyperDoc or HyperSlides, which can order the lectures in a progression for students to interact with through a specific order. Lastly, edtech tools like Edpuzzle can be used concurrently with your edited screencasts where questions can be added by teachers to break up the lecture to check their student's comprehension of the material as the student moves through the lecture content.

Class or Small Group Student Brainstorming and Collaboration. Online collaboration or brainstorming can take many different forms. For example, a Google Doc can be shared with an entire class on a learning management system like Google Classroom, where the class can collaborate on and have access to all editable documents. Or, similarly, it can be shared directly through a hyperlink on a HyperDoc or a HyperSlide for students to access the editable document.

In a different manner for smaller groups, a teacher or a student can share a Google Doc with their group mates, which only gives those specific students editing rights on the document. Another method for students to collaborate is on Padlet, which gives students an entire digital bulletin board to share their thoughts on a given topic. Students can share text, images, audio recordings, and videos, which provide many different modalities of learning as well as mediums to articulate and demonstrate learning.

Lastly, Flipgrid allows for students to work together in small groups or an entire class to collaborate or brainstorm. For example, when a teacher presents a prompt on the content, students can answer this prompt through their initial Flipgrid recorded response. Then, afterward, students can listen and respond to selected students for a small group activity or list to at least one-third of the class and then provide a written response.

Activating Prior Knowledge. Activating prior knowledge allows our students to utilize what they already know to help create a knowledge foundation on the content or skill being taught by their teacher (Dikkers et al., 2017, p. 160). Doing this in an online setting can be done using a frontloading approach or a scaffolded approach. A frontloading approach can be best illustrated by providing students with a hook leading in tandem with a large bulk of the content to build a foundational association with the content. In an online class setting, this could be the use of video content like found on Classhooks, of the content being alluded to or depicted on a TV sitcom. Or, correspondingly, a YouTube video can be used that has been edited using Edpuzzle or Loom to ask students multiple-choice, open-ended, or summarization review questions as the video progresses to activate their thought processes and working memory.

Another example of prior knowledge could be a Flipgrid teacher recorded response, which depicts a teacher modeling a think-aloud. Within this clip, the teacher asks their students to record their think-aloud on the topic at hand. After their initial first response, students then can respond to several of their classmate's think-aloud to develop an ongoing discussion to activate prior knowledge on the topic further as the conversation progresses. This is an example of how students and teachers alike can create purposeful interactions and provides opportunities to connect with their classmates and teachers to learn more about a topic in an online or blended learning educational setting (Whiteside & Dikkers, 2015).

Scaffolding Content. For scaffolding content to work effectively as an instructional strategy for online and blended learning, it can be embedded within synchronous and asynchronous lessons (Institute of Education Sciences, 2008). An example of this in action could be using an interactive slideshow where students are required to fill in various parts of it for notes. For example, if the content is on the Civil War, the first slide could be a link to a video on the content students must respond to in their response. Then, the next slide could be a graphic organizer in the form of a KWL or a Notice, Wonder, and, Know Chart where students must complete as they read and interact with the materials posted in the slideshow (Steele, 2014). At the end of the slideshow, students can respond to a writing prompt or be connected to a short assessment through a hyperlink to a Google Form, Quizzizz, Kahoot, or a GoFormative quiz.

Conversely, a teacher can present a prompt associated with a video that has been attached to a document, which would be utilizing the Think-Write-Pair-Share instructional strategy (Tanujaya & Mumu, 2019). Ultimately, the directions would tell the students they must watch the video, think, respond to the prompt, and then share their response in the form of a recorded video to at least two of their classmates. Then, their classmates must respond to them in the form of an email or recorded video, students then revise their post, and then post it for the entire class to read or view on Google Classroom.

Active Participation during Synchronous Live Sessions. During synchronous sessions, the active participation of your students during the session is important to maintaining their engagement. One of the ways to ensure students are participating is to build a Google Slides presentation with the add-on Pear Deck application. With Pear Deck, you can build interactive slideshows where students must respond to polls, multiple-choice questions, free-response questions, and drawing/draggable questions. In practice during a synchronous session, a teacher will share students the URL to where they can access the live slideshow. Then, instead of a teacher sharing their screen during the live synchronous session, students are viewing the live Pear Deck slideshow. As a result, the teacher on the backend of Pear Deck during the synchronous sessions can be presenting information as well as evaluating whether their students are engaged and answering the questions presented so they can assess their student's learning.

By utilizing active learning as a strategy with Pear Deck, you can ensure your synchronous sessions are worthwhile for two reasons. First, teachers can collect valuable data on student engagement (i.e., who participated in today's live class session). Second, student formative assessment data can be collected by teachers as short quizzes can be built into your Pear Deck slide to see how students are doing in real-time. Ultimately, by utilizing Pear Deck for your online live synchronous sessions, teachers can bolster active participation and student engagement. Through the integration of this tool, it will help students be more inclined to understand your directions for the content and asynchronous portions of your online class.

Summarization/Review. Summarization and review of content can be done in a multitude of ways. By summarizing and reviewing what has been covered, students can reflect and bring forth central ideas they have learned to future units of study (Afflerbach et al., 2020). Additionally, teachers can review their students' summaries and determine if any content gaps must be filled through the re-teaching of content. Asynchronously, at the end of your slideshow, a link to a Google Form can be provided to students for them to summarize the lessons key points and self-assess what they have learned. The names of the students, as well as their summaries, are recorded for the teacher to review. Another way to do this could include either a Google Doc or Slideshow, which can be posted as an assignment where students must develop their own infographic or slideshow that summarizes the major concepts discussed in the lesson or unit. Lastly, a teacher can instruct students to build a digital portfolio for the class over the semester. Google Sites, Wordpress, Square Space, or Weebly are great website interfaces students can use to build a website that summaries their learning. Additionally, it can be used as an interface and storage cloud exhibiting the skills learned in a class by students for allowing them to post/link student-created artifacts they have completed. Furthermore, included in these digital website portfolios, teachers can instruct students to write a short blog post summarizing what they have learned in the unit of study. As you can see, there is a multitude of options available for teachers to instruct their students to summarize their learning.

In a synchronous session, a teacher can employ Pear Deck and have students answer several free-response questions asking them to summarize their learning. Or, in a similar fashion, using Pear Deck or an application like Poll Everywhere, teachers can pose a multiple-choice or open-ended question(s) that relates to the major themes discussed in a unit or lesson. Then, once the class is completed by answering these questions, the teacher can create breakout rooms or have a full class discussion on the questions to further dig deeper into the student answers.

Metacognition. Metacognition provides an opportunity for students to reflect on their progress through critical thinking and assessing how they feel through socio-emotional learning (Hartman, 2001). It is critical for teachers to gauge their students' learning through the reflection process as well as evaluate where individual students and the class are socio-emotionally (Farley & Lare, 2012). This is especially important now during this crisis as well as in the months and years after because it allows students to be reflective learners and critical thinkers to adapt to their ever-changing surroundings.

In practice, metacognition can take several forms. For example, a teacher can develop a survey on Google Forms (or SurveyMonkey, Formative, etc.) that allows students to answer on a weekly basis, which asks them a multitude of questions prompting them to reflect on their progress academically and socio-emotionally. Questions presented can ask students how much they understood the content, whether they liked how the information was presented, assessing how students feel about what was covered, and how they can apply the information to real-life applications (Farley & Lare, 2012). These types of questions are great starters for metacognition exercises.

Besides a weekly survey, teachers can ask their students socio-emotional and reflection questions that require metacognition on a Google Docs and student-built slides assignment in Google Classroom (or another learning management system that may be in use). Lastly, during synchronous live sessions, interactive slides like Pear Deck can have several prebuilt reflection/socio-emotional questions into its interface, which teachers can quickly add to their slideshow. Therefore, when students answer these questions, teachers have a live stream of answers to gauge where the class and individual students are socio-emotionally.

Assessment. Formative and summative assessments (i.e., real-time or at the end of the lesson quizzes and exams after a unit of study(allow teachers to determine if their students have a grasp on the content or skills taught in their class regardless of the educational setting. For online learning and face to face settings, teachers can develop formative and summative assessments using Google Forms, b.socrativ, and Formative. On these platforms, teachers can use prebuilt assessments on the content or build their own assessments and align them to standards. Each of these edtech tools provides teachers to ask a multitude of questions ranging from multiple-choice, free response, and drag and drop multiple-choice questions. What's great about these tools is that student data is created once students complete the assessments, which then can be exported to a spreadsheet. Additionally, there are data visualizations regarding the types of questions students answered correctly vs. incorrectly. By analyzing the collected data from the entire class, individual students, and question types, it allows teachers to monitor and adjust instruction and provide additional support for students if needed.

For writing assignments, teachers can create rubrics on Google Forms, Google Classroom, or other learning management systems such as Blackboard and Canvas to assess student learning. Rubrics on learning management systems take the rubric grades and transfer them to the grade book, which makes grading writing much more efficient in terms of the time it takes logistically to enter grades.

During synchronous live sessions, teachers can use Pear Deck to assess their student's responses live during the session using multiple-choice or free-response questions. Teachers can view the student responses collectively as a class or for individual students. As a result, teachers can then monitor and adjust their instruction, if needed.

Weekly Lesson Plan Outline Example

Now, after seeing how various instructional strategies that can be used in a face to face setting, and within an online classroom setting using a variety of edtech tools, it's time to see how weekly lessons can be developed for online learning. Similarly, this template can also be employed for a blended learning model whereby the online synchronous sessions turn into face to face classroom instruction. When viewing the template presented, teachers can utilize this template by inserting the content/skills they would like to build into the lesson outline for the week. Throughout the lesson plan template, office hours are built into two days when students are doing their work asynchronously so they can receive additional support from their teacher.

Monday: Synchronous Sessions - Pear Deck Slides, Checking in with Students, Reviewing the Week's Asynchronous Directions. Pear Deck slides include socio-emotional check-in questions, assignment direction review questions, and a quick write responding to a prompt or video prompt.

Tuesday - Wednesday: Asynchronous - Content Frontload and Interactive Discussion Board. Students will have a Google Slideshow to fill out self-guided/independently posted on the learning management system. This slideshow will include hyperlinks to documents and videos relating to the content they are learning. In various areas of the slideshow, students must provide a written response, which may include completing several graphic organizers. Once students have completed the slideshow, students will be required to participate in an online discussion board using Flipgrid. Within Flipgrid, students will be required to respond to the initial prompt and then be asked to respond to at least two to three of their classmates.

Office Hours: 1:00 - 2:00 p.m.

Wednesday - Thursday: Asynchronous - Student Assignment; Student Created Work Product. Students will be asked to take the content they interacted with on Tuesday/Wednesday to create a student work product. This assignment can be posted in your learning management system. In these assignments, you can give your students a choice to create a work product that incorporates the content discussed during the first three days of the week. Teachers can provide students with the assignments choices to develop their own blog post, video recording, infographic, three - five-paragraph essay/response to a prompt, etc. There are many choices teachers can choose here based on their grade level, content, and student population. This assignment can be due Sunday at midnight or Friday at midnight, depending on the teacher's preference.

Office Hours: 1:00-2:00 p.m.

Thursday – Friday: Asynchronous/Synchronous - Assessment and Review. During these days, a teacher can assess their students' learning by posting a teacher-built assessment on their learning management system that gives students a testing window to complete during a given time. Once the assessment window is closed, a synchronous live class session can take place on Friday to review the results with students as well as re-teach any concepts within the content that need to be re-taught. Another method of assessment could take place in the live synchronous session where the teacher provides various assessment questions on Pear Deck, which their students will answer. Then, based on the assessment results, the teacher can address specific questions students need further instruction on the content.

Conclusion

Throughout this conversation, we hope we have been able to illustrate how we can align the various face to face instructional strategies to the edtech tools we are using for our online and blended learning classes. In the end, it takes some time and thought, but on many levels, much of what we do in our face to face classes can be transferred over to online and blended learning educational settings. We also hope the week-long lesson plan outline helps provide insight at how to plan on a weekly basis for a class. In terms of the balance between synchronous and asynchronous instruction, we suggest regardless of grade level one to two days synchronous live sessions last between thirty minutes to an hour-long. When schools begin opening, synchronous time will increase depending on schedule protocols and grade level. Then, in regards to asynchronous instruction, we recommend three to four days a week and by giving students two to four hours of instruction/work depending on the grade level. Ultimately, for teachers to be successful in this format, it will require several hours upfront to build a weekly lesson. A benefit of being in this type of format is it provides teachers the freedom to plan several weeks ahead, create more flexible schedules to develop content, to work with students during live sessions, to communicate with students/parents, to assess student work and assessments, and to have office hours.

Part 1. Conclusion

Throughout the last four chapters, we have been able to see how teachers and administrators can build and refine their district and schools' online infrastructures. We covered selecting what edtech tools that may best fit a teacher's content, grade level, and student population. We further built upon this by providing information about mainstream edtech tools and their applications to learning. This ultimately added up to provide the steps required for creating an effective online learning classroom that can toggle back and forth between online and blended learning models. Lastly, we covered how to integrate face to face instructional strategies with edtech tools we can utilize in online learning and blended learning educational settings. This conversation also discussed how to create weekly lesson plans that provided templates for synchronous and asynchronous instruction. Now, with a solid understanding of edtech and online instruction in place, we can focus on maximizing our instruction during synchronous sessions, communicating and engaging parents and students with online learning, differentiating instruction for students with special needs, and how to case manage students enrolled in Special Education in addition to conducting IEP meetings online. Understanding each of these components is essential to secondary schools because they must be further developed and refined for the fall semester in addition to being able to provide the critical option to toggle back and forth between online and face to face learning.

PART 2

Maximizing Synchronous Instruction, Parent & Student Engagement and Communication, Differentiated Instruction, and Navigating Special Education

With a solid foundation in place, it is time to expand our horizons. There are many additional areas teachers and administrators need to have knowledge in so we can begin to think about how to develop plans to reopen schools for the fall and to be able to navigate the reality of a toggled term. We have to think about maximizing synchronous instruction as well as engaging and communicating with parents and students to get them fully involved and to buy-in to the instructional model that will be in place. Additionally, we must be ready to develop plans with students with special needs in mind. What this includes is differentiating instruction in online and blended learning, case managing students in an online setting, and holding IEP meetings online.

Within this part of the book, four chapters address these critical areas. First, we want to be sure we can bolster our synchronous instruction as it will eventually move from online live sessions to face to face sessions. Second, conversations will shift towards engaging and communicating parents and students during online learning. We cannot have successful online or blended learning environments without engagement and participation from students and their families.

Going further, we must focus on students with special needs as they are the student population that will need the most support in the event of a toggled term where parts of the semester will be fully online or within a blended learning setting. Understanding how to differentiate instruction by secondary teachers and administrators for online instruction will help us adapt IEP's to instruction in both an online and blended learning educational setting that can benefit these students. Lastly, navigating Special Education case managing and IEP meetings during a toggled term will ensure schools are doing their best to maintain compliance with the student IEP process and the Individuals with Disability Education Act (IDEA).

Our hope going forward is for teachers and administrators to have a solid foundation in supporting all of our students, especially students who need the highest level of support within online and in face to face educational settings. Overall, this will ultimately look like a blended learning education setting, but we know there will be times schools will have to switch back and forth depending on our local conditions. Therefore, be ready to continue learning to build your repertoire of strategies to maximize your understanding of how we support our students.

CHAPTER 5

Maximizing Live Synchronous Class Sessions and Google Meet - Strategies to Help Bolster Your Student's Online Learning

As our transition to online learning occurred in the spring of 2020, the platforms used by many districts and schools to hold synchronous live class sessions included **Google Meet**, **Zoom**, **AdobeConnect**, and **Microsoft Teams**. During these online synchronous class sessions, instruction over time can begin to mirror face to face instruction, in some regards, as many of the same instructional strategies, as mentioned earlier in Chapter 4, began to be more commonplace. One of the most popular meeting platforms, Google Meet, is a platform offered through Google's G-Suite, which allows for live video conferencing of up to 200 people. Since Google Meet is one of the most used K-12 online synchronous online meeting tools available (along with Zoom and Microsoft Teams), we are going to begin our conversation with how to optimize Google Meet for synchronous classes. Then, our goal of this chapter is to focus on providing several essential strategies to maximize synchronous instruction online while being mindful that these classes may ease into face to face synchronous class sessions. With the help of these strategies, we want teachers to integrate as many of them as possible into their synchronous class sessions. Ultimately, these strategies are considered best practices by many experts in the field. Additionally, we want administrators to learn about these strategies to be able to coach their teachers on how to implement them in their synchronous online classrooms as well as be ready for the eventual transition to synchronous face to face class sessions.

Integration of Google Meet with Google Classroom and Helpful Extensions

Google Meet is a vital platform for synchronous online class instruction. It allows teachers to share content through the ongoing chat feature and to share their screen with students. The share screen option gives teachers the ability to present a wide range of presentations for their students to interact with during class sessions. During the spring of 2020, Google Meet was integrated into Google Classroom. This development made it a very efficient process to launch a live Google Meet live session link from the Google Classroom "stream" home page interface. To incorporate Google Meet for a synchronous class session, all a teacher must do is to go to the settings toolbox after entering a designated classroom. Once Google Meet has been activated through the settings, a link appears in the Google Classroom heading on the "stream" homepage with the Meet link students can click, which brings them directly to the online Google Meet class session.

Beyond Google Classroom, there are two extensions teachers and students need to download to maximize Google Meet's potential for live class sessions fully. First, teachers and students must add the extension of "**Google Meet Grid View**," which allows both teachers and students to see everyone's video image in the live class session. Within this feature, each student is shown within a grid view, which shows every classmate's profile picture or live webcam when it's been added as an extension. Without this extension, a grid view of an entire class is not possible, so teachers nor their students can see everyone's video image at once while class is live. Second, teachers and students are encouraged to add the extension "**Nod - Reactions for Google Meet**," which allows both teachers and students to raise a virtual hand as well as display various emojis such as a thumbs up or thumbs down to the entire live class session.

Further integrations are coming in the summer of 2020 for Google Meet. These new integrations and features include break out rooms, digital whiteboards, meeting moderation controls (hosts are provided more options to mute, invite, etc.), take attendance option, background blur for teachers and students, the raising hand feature, and polling and question options. All of these updates align with the new and current features of Zoom and Microsoft Teams.

Ultimately, with the ability to integrate Google Meet into Google Classroom as well as adding the Grid View and Nod Reactions extensions to Google Meet along with the new updated features, it creates an effective platform to conduct online synchronous meetings. With these features in place, teachers have options to create engagement meetings for their students as well as seek non-verbal and verbal feedback while they are presenting content to their students during screen sharing mode. This allows for participation within a class to be overt and covert as different forms of learning occur, as well as provide a more engaging learning environment.

Online Strategies to Maximize Live Synchronous Sessions

When conducting live online synchronous class sessions through Google Meet (or Microsoft Teams or Zoom), there are many strategies to maximize your class time as a teacher and student learning. Below, we have provided a list of **10 successful strategies** utilized by teachers to help bolster your students' learning and your time as a teacher during live synchronous sessions.

- **Mute Microphones:** Ask students to mute their microphones once the meeting begins. Having background noise can be distracting to the teacher as well as students. By ensuring this is a clear expectation from the beginning will help mitigate unnecessary background noises.

- **Agenda/Goals:** Provide a daily agenda and learning goals on the first slide you are sharing with the class. Then, review it with your students before jumping into the full lesson. This provides structure and allows your students to know what you will be covering during this live class session and learning throughout the week.

- **Etiquette Online:** Review online class etiquette. For example, what are the procedures for raising your virtual hand or providing insight either in the chatbox or by explaining their thoughts using their voice? These procedures to be set in the first few class sessions. Lastly, be sure to note that the chatbox is being logged, so students need to be appropriate in their use of language and interactions with students.

- **Check-in with your Students:** When checking in with your students, you can either ask them to write a number out of ten representing how they feel or use interactive slides like Pear Deck to poll them on how they are feeling interactively. Teachers can also ask them to use an emoji to illustrate how they are doing once students have downloaded the "Nod" extension. Then, during this time, teachers can virtually call on two to three students virtually after they have initially checked in with the entire class to allow these students to share their thoughts with their voice to the rest of the class. Be sure to have your students raise their virtual hand to volunteer while in your online class.

- **Early in the Week Live Class Sessions:** For live sessions at the beginning of the week, go over the content you have posted online and review the instructions. Frontload as much as possible. Lastly, ask students multiple times if they have any questions and remind them about signing up for office hours throughout the week. By ensuring all questions are answered upfront is critical to assess whether students fully understand the directions for the week.

- **Later in the Week Live Class Sessions:** For sessions at the end of the week, review content and re-teach as needed. During these sessions, it's best to review what has been covered as well as provide feedback directly to the entire class or target students. If an assessment has occurred, go over the problems, tasks, or problems that students had the most trouble with and answer any questions regarding their confusion to bridge their understanding.

- **Online Lectures/Direct Instruction:** For sessions that may involve a lecture and direct instruction, use interactive slides like **Pear Deck** or **Poll Everywhere** extensions with your Google Slideshows to engage your students in active participation actively. By providing live opinion polls, formative assessment questions, and interactive visuals, it helps maintain student engagement during a live online lecture. Remember,the same edtech tools and strategies can be used during a face to face class session in the same manner.

- **Office Hours:** Always remind your students about virtual office hours and how to sign up for them. This is huge as many students may want one on one support or may not want to ask questions during agroup setting regarding the content being reviewed in class. Also, office hours provide a medium to build relationships with students online as it gives you and the student time to work together and collaborate on their learning.

- **Take Virtual Attendance:** Have a Google Form, Doc, or have your IT department modify your student information system to track your student's attendance and participation during online or blended learning. If you have to use a Google Form or Doc, be sure to have the date, class period, the number of students missing, and the names of the students missing. This will allow you to contact students who have missed one or more live class sessions to check-in and see how they are doing.

- **Be Engaging and Have Fun:** While presenting to your students, have some energy in your voice. By having excitement and zest in your voice will allow your students to become more engaged in the live lesson. With anything in life, the energy that you are expressing through your voice and actions will help create more energy for your class session.

Conclusion

Online synchronous classes are much different than face to face in terms of their feel and setting. Teachers can make these live class sessions effective in many of the same ways as they would in face to face class sessions by using the strategies provided. Teachers can also integrate many of the teaching practices they used during their face to face classes within the online setting. This is essential to know as instruction will eventually be easing into face to face class sessions or toggling back and forth between online and blended learning environments. Additionally, be aware that there may be scenarios where half of the students are tuning online, while the other half are attending face to face. Thus, teachers will be in a position where they will have to teach through multiple mediums and remain engaging. Teachers know this is possible and can be done effectively.

At the end of the day, this will take practice as well as time to refine a teacher's ability to teach an engaging synchronous online class session. Ultimately, all educators, regardless of their experience in online or blended learning, are improving in conducting online lessons. Over time, if teachers and administrators follow and implement the strategies discussed for online synchronous sessions, the easing into blended learning models will transition without too much turbulence.

CHAPTER 6

Student and Parental Engagement for Online Learning - Building Community Online through Edtech

As classes and entire schools transitioned online in the early spring, building a community was vital to stay connected with students and parents. Student and parent engagement continues to be one of the most essential facets teachers and administrators need to strive to achieve in their districts and school communities (Borup, Stevens, & Waters, 2015). Simply put, students want to hear and see their teacher and stay connected with their classmates regardless of their educational setting. Humans need connections and relationships as it is within our nature to be social and build connections with others.

As a result, this chapter will spend additional time reviewing several edtech tools and strategies to help teachers and administrators stay connected with their students as well as provide opportunities for students to stay connected with their classmates. Beyond this discussion, time will be allocated to discuss how teachers can facilitate parental involvement in their student's learning with online classrooms through various means of communication. Through this conversation, we hope that you will see the power of communication and how it builds a community for online learners, which will heighten student participation and engagement in your online classroom. Furthermore, it will also prepare teachers and administrators to have two-facet communities at the beginning of the fall semester: one online community, and one face to face community. These two communities need to be nurtured and synthesized as much as possible before schools begin the process of reopening and navigating the toggled term. Ultimately, in all likelihood, this will be our reality going forward for at least the next semester or even the entire school year.

Teachers Staying Connected to Students Online - Building an Online Community through Communication

Teachers have several options to maintain communication with students. The easiest method is to email each of their students in their classes. On email platforms like Gmail, teachers can develop templates and schedule daily and weekly emails to their students. Emailing students in this manner can also take place on learning management systems like **Google Classroom**, **Schoology**, and **Canvas**. To obtain your student's email addresses, student emails can be found on your student information system. In terms of the contents of these emails, teachers can provide the daily/weekly schedule, inspirational quotes, weekly video updates, images, memes, infographics, and gifs, and may even provide a personal update about what is going on in their life. These forms of communication align with Borup, Graham, and Drysdale's (2013) findings regarding how teachers should provide multiple methods of communication to reach students for online and blended learning educational settings. On this note, be sure to ensure all emails are bcc'ed to maintain the anonymity of the email addresses of your students. Remember, at the end of the day, all of these topics shared through email or any other forms of virtual communication are important to touch on as it builds a connection with your students and establishes a schedule/routine with them concerning your online and eventual blended learning classroom.

Another method to stay connected with students is through online discussion boards. Traditional discussion boards can be developed in many learning management systems. However, with all schools going to online learning during this crisis, we believe students seeing and hearing their classmate's voices is critical to continuing an online community. Thus, to do this, **Flipgrid** is one of the best free edtech tools available to develop an engaging and interactive online discussion board that utilizes video and audio for students to respond to prompts presented by their teacher. Then, Flipgrid provides an opportunity for students to watch and listen to their classmates and then respond to them. In this type of virtual discussion board, having all students seeing and hearing their teacher and classmates powerful for building community and promoting higher-level thinking beyond similar opportunities to communicate while meeting for a live online or face to face synchronous class session (O'Brien et al., 2014). Overall, by using a tool like Flipgrid, it may heighten an entire class's engagement and sense of community through their participation.

Outside of emails and online discussion boards, teachers can create their own interactive infographic/online posters to keep in contact with students and parents. This graphic can include an embedded video, hyperlinks to resources, an image relating to the week's learning themes, and text, which could include an inspiration quote, schedule, or a short paragraph outlining important bulletins students and parents need to know about for the week. An infographic/ online poster like this can be built on **Google Slides**, **PowerPoint**, **Canva**, **Photoshop**, **Padlet**, and within many other edtech tools. To distribute this infographic/online poster, it can be sent via email or posted on a learning management system for students and parents to view when needed throughout the week.

Lastly, teachers can communicate their students in a variety of different ways. Teachers can communicate with their students by email, by posting a daily or weekly video message outlining the day's/ week's schedule on their learning management system, during live synchronous class sessions or office hours, or by texting or calling students and families through Google Voice. By providing a video message or some form of daily check-in to communicate with students, it gives students an immediate connection with their teacher. Also, by providing a regular video message, students get to see and hear their teacher, which builds and continues the connection with students while enduring a semester where students may toggle back and forth between online and face to face instruction. Ultimately, sustaining relationships with students is vital for their engagement and participation in the learning taking place within online and blended settings (Borup et al., 2013). Thus, when teachers and administrators check in with their students in meaningful ways, students will be engaged in school and do better in their courses.

Teachers Staying Connected with Parents - Building Community through Transparency with Parents

Like with students, teachers need to continue building connections with parents (Harris & Goodall, 2008). The easiest way to continue this connection is through consistently emailing, texting, and calling parents when needed to keep them in the loop regarding their students' progress. We recommend teachers send out the same weekly emails or online infographics/online posters they send to their students and their student's parents. What this does is establish transparency between students, parents, and the teacher. As a result, each party then has the resources to understand what is going on and has a general idea of what's going on in the online or within a blended learning classroom regarding the weekly expectations for students.

In all likelihood, teachers will have to 'toggle' back and forth from their school site and home to teach through the 2020-2021 school year and possibly beyond. In this scenario, teachers may have a hard time calling parents because they do not have a work phone at home or a district-issued cell phone. Luckily, there is a solution with the help of edtech. If teachers want to call their student's parents, **Google Voice** is a fantastic service that allows teachers to call and text parents using a private number that is not a personal phone number. Google Voice can be downloaded as a smartphone application or utilized on a personal computer through a web browser, which allows teachers to use Google Voice on their laptops and smartphones as mediums to use the free service. One of the features that are incredibly valuable with Google Voice is its ability to record voice calls, voice messages, and log text conversations. This is an important mechanism to document conversations with parents at one point in time or over the long haul. Ultimately, what makes Google Voice such a powerful communication tool during this crisis is that Google Voice allows teachers to have a work phone number that can be used while they work from home.

Conclusion

Building community and maintaining communication with students and parents is essential to maintaining engagement and participation in online and blended learning classrooms. Without engagement and connection, the levels of participation among students will be lower than what we want to have an inclusive and prosperous classroom for our students. Therefore, building and maintaining an online community that can also be transferable to face to face is critical for instances of when schools allow face to face classrooms to occur as well as when schools will have to toggle back to online instruction. But more importantly, this community building and communication must be consistent over time, especially during times of transition between online and blended learning. By communicating often, it ensures students and parents are plugged into the class, school, and district happenings on a daily and weekly basis. Also, this will be a proactive measure in maintaining student, teacher, and staff safety because it will be up to the school community to be accountable for new protocols implemented for the fall. Lastly, in the same manner, the school community will be essential in smooth transitions between online and blended learning because the communication systems and relationships will be in place between teachers and students. This will be the cultural fabric of whether any transition will be successful back towards face to face blended learning model or back fully to online learning will be tumultuous or without many hiccups.

CHAPTER 7

Differentiated Instruction - Online Instruction for Special Education and English Language Learners

Transitioning directly to online education is a considerable undertaking and transition. Once our classroom is built online and functioning, we need to think about instruction, but also in that same breath, differentiated instruction should be for all who have special needs as well as our English Language Learners (ELL). We previously discussed earlier in this book how to incorporate instruction strategies alongside our edtech. Now, we want to expand our instructional know-how and tool kit to focus on how we can differentiate instruction for students with Individualized Education Plans (IEPs) and English Language Learners (ELL) within online and blended learning classroom settings. As a result, much of what we are going to discuss is how we can embed differentiated instruction into the content we create within these educational settings for reading, writing, and mathematics. This is consistent with research regarding how our online and blended learning course designs need to meet the needs of all learning (Keeler & Horney, 2007). Additionally, during this conversation, we will focus on illustrating how we can demonstrate our creativity and develop alternative assignments and tasks that we can specifically assign to individual students or groups of students that may need further support. Thus, through differentiated instruction, teachers can design and build online and blended learning classrooms for students of all ability levels so they can be engaged and to be able to interact with the content and skills we are teaching.

Special Education & English Language Learner Online Supports

Before speaking more specifically about embedding supports within your content you are creating to differentiate your instruction, we want to touch on a number of factors we want teachers and administrators to consider while providing instruction for students who receive Special Education services and ELL's in your classroom. To address the needs of all learners in addition to students enrolled in Special Education and ELL's, we have developed five components we want you to first focus on while setting up or refining your online and blended learning classroom.

Set and Model Clear Expectations and Routines. First, we want to set and model clear expectations and routines. This is especially true for online and blended learning because setting and modeling expectations provide structure and routines for students regardless of their educational setting (Butcher & Wilson-Strydom, 2008). What this means is to initially show your students through guided lecture videos or during your initial synchronous live class sessions how your online classroom's learning management system functions. To facilitate having students learn the class expectations, it means going through everyday routines for the online classroom and learning management system to ensure your students understand how it functions. For example, these routines can include showing how students turn in work, where students access the weekly information slideshow and course content, how to access the classroom calendar, providing opportunities to review the edtech tools you will be using at first in addition to your learning management system, outline where to access resources like a syllabus that illustrate the expectations for online and blended learning classrooms, and the options of how to communicate with their teacher. All of these facets are critical to our student's understanding of what to do when interacting with online content in a primarily online setting or within a blended learning educational setting. Going further, if districts allow synchronous sessions to be recorded, record your synchronous sessions reviewing these expectations and routines or post guided lecture screencasts on learning management systems for students to have resources to view if they need a refresher in these areas.

Chunk Content as Much as Possible. Second, teachers need to chunk tasks, assignments, and content as much as possible, regardless of their grade level, to scaffold instruction (Drexler, 2010). For online and a blended learning class, the chunking and scaffolding of content are vital to help students organize content, synthesize ideas, taking responsibility for their learning, collaboration with peers, working with technology, and practicing digital literacy and responsibility (Drexler, 2010). For all of these facets, teachers must explain the directions and provide modeling to their students; they need to be sure to chunk and scaffold their content as much. Asynchronously, teachers need to ensure when they screencast or post video content, the shorter the videos, the better.

Additionally, while teachers are editing their screencasts, they can make segments of the video by providing signposts signifying the steps they are on. Applications like **Edpuzzle**, **CommonLit**, and **Loom** allow for teachers to provide comprehension questions to gauge student learning. Also, teachers need to note that within their class slideshows, online documents, or on class bulletins on their learning management system, they should chunk their content. Ultimately, teachers do not need to put everything on one page and have it too dense with text.Instead, a step by step process is much more accessible and easier to understand for students.

Incrementally Scaffold Textual Directions. Third, teachers need to scaffold tasks, assignments, and units of study incrementally (Drexler, 2010). Again, this relates to chunking content but in a different way. For example, what we mean here is that with textual instructions, teachers need to write down step by step directions when they are providing students with assignment directions on slides, on a document, or through email. Teachers can also highlight various steps with different colors to signify what students must do for each color on the page.

Foster Online Verbal Discussions to Develop Community. Fourth, teachers need to provide opportunities for verbal class discussions and opportunities to check in with students synchronously and asynchronously (Drexler, 2010). At least once or twice per week, we recommend teachers dedicate a short segment of their synchronous live session to check in with their entire class or ensure students visit teachers at least once a week for office hours. Also, utilize a platform like Flipgrid or backchannel edtech tools like YoTeach! can be used to develop online discussions among your students on the content they are working on or regarding apersonal topic of their choice. Through these mediums, students can respond via video, audio, or multimedia to their teacher(s) and classmates, which allows them still to maintain some form of communication with their classmates.

Provide Feedback through Email, Comments on Students Assignments on the Learning Management System, Audio Feedback, and Video. Fifth, teachers need to provide as much feedback as possible on student assignments and tasks to ensure the learning process is continuous in an online or blended learning environment. Liu and Cavanaugh (2011) outline how teachers must be actively involved in providing quality feedback to students in an online and blended educational setting to ensure active learning is occurring. Thus, teachers need to be available to their students to provide feedback through a variety of different mediums. That does not mean teachers have to reply to their questions immediately. What this means is they should respond via email, commenting on assignments, or by a video or embedded audio response during the school day to provide quality feedback to their students.

Additionally, this feedback can also take the form of providing entire class feedback, group feedback, or individual student feedback. To this end, it will ultimately depend on the scenario. Most importantly, teacher availability to provide feedback is a valuable action they can do when online or in a blended learning classroom to ensure active learning is taking place (Liu & Cavanuagh, 2011).

Differentiated Reading, Writing, and Mathematics Supports

Now, beyond providing the components that are required to provide some form of embedded differentiated instruction within the design of the course and curriculum, we are going to focus specifically on various content areas teachers can further differentiate instruction. While thinking of content differentiation, be sure to evaluate the overarching differentiation techniques of increasing student time on the task, providing varied groupings of students, scaffolded instruction, and the gradual release of responsibility when developing your lesson plans (Institute of Education Sciences, 2008). Furthermore, for each content area of reading, writing, and math, we will be providing several examples of how to differentiate instruction as well as provide embedded support in these areas. We hope that each of these strategies and supports to differentiate can be utilized for both Special Education and ELL students.

Differentiation Supports for Reading

One of the easiest ways to differentiate reading for your students is to show your students how to utilize the read-aloud function on Google Docs as well as how to highlight and comment text on the documents interface. Once this groundwork has been completed, create two types of documents; the original document students will interact with and a **Rewordify** document. Rewordify is a tool that allows teachers to copy and paste their reading passage into the software, which then reconfigures the difficult words/phrases of the passage and transforms them into words/phrases students at a third to fifth-grade reading level can understand. Thus, with two documents, students can refer to the original document to highlight, paraphrase, and annotate digitally, and then have another document they can refer to help them in interacting with the document they are reading. Lastly, **Google Read and Write** is a paid-for extension schools can buy that supports students reading by providing images, vocabulary definitions/images, and read-alouds to students to help break down a complex text. For the best optimization of this is tool is to have all students have access to this extension. Ultimately, Google Read and Write can provide many supports to help students comprehend and evaluate texts in a multitude of modalities (i.e., reading, seeing, and hearing).

Another great way to differentiate reading instruction online is to use adaptive software to meet students at their current reading level. **Readtheory**, **Achieve 3000**, **Read 180**, and **Freckle** are all web-based applications that initially assess your student's reading levels and then provide instruction based on the student's areas of strength and improvement. Thus, once they are done assessing a student's reading levels, their reading lessons and passages will adapt to the student's reading levels. Adaptive reading software can be used to guide one on one instruction to students provided by their teacher. They can also be used for independent practice activities where students can do daily and weekly practice on their reading comprehension skills such as finding the main idea, key details, passage structure and syntax, and the synthesizing information from the text.

Differentiated Supports for Writing

Writing exercises can be differentiated through a multitude of different avenues. For Google Docs, speech-to-text is one of the first tools students can become familiar with when using the application. Speech-to-text allows students to begin writing out sentences before going back to revise them. Then, to provide support to help students edit and revise their written sentences, we recommend that teachers have your students download the free **Grammarly** extension to Google Docs, which is an AI-based grammar/punctuation revision application. Through this extension, students can see where they have made grammatical or punctuation errors in their writing when Grammarly is enabled. Thus, through this process, it allows students to see their mistakes and then see how to correct them. Over time with practice, it will help students learn from their mistakes and write more proficiently.

Another avenue teachers can take to differentiate writing is to build sentence frames into the documents they want their students to complete their writing assignments. For various groups of students, the sentence frames can be more guided and less guided, depending on the students' writing needs and ability. This can be done by assigning the differentiated assignments on their learning management system with the differing levels of sentence frames to targeted students to meet them where they currently are in their writing. Many learning management systems like Google Classroom and Seesaw allow teachers to assign different assignments to individual students or groups of students without having to assign the task or assignment to the entire class.

Lastly, we wanted to discuss the importance of teachers using the revision/comment feature on Google Docs to provide students with feedback during the writing process. For online and blended learning, ongoing written feedback is vital as it can provide students several examples of areas they need to improve. Also, revision/comment feedback on student writing can be considered points of emphasis to discuss during office hours or a synchronous live class.

Differentiated Supports for Math

Differentiated math instruction online and blended learning classrooms can be tricky, but completely doable. First, provide multiple video tutorials of how a particular type of problem is solved. For example, if you are teaching students how to do linear equations, provide at least three short videos that show step by step of how they are solved. Additionally, teachers should be encouraged to develop multiple screencasts of how a single math problem can be solved in two or more ways. With screencasting tools like **Screencastify, Loom**, or **Screencast-O-Matic**, teachers can record their screen on a whiteboard tool like **Whiteboard Fox, Sketchboard**, and **Jamboard** to do guided math instruction. Students can then review the recorded video as much as they would like at their own pace. Similarly, the same whiteboards can be used for live synchronous class sessions and for collaborating with students during office hours. Students can follow along on the same digital whiteboards individually or collaboratively with their classmates, or they can use traditional paper and pencil and watch their teachers model math instruction.

Another method to differentiate math instruction is to provide different groups of students in your class with step by step graphics of how problems are solved in their independent practice assignments. Graphics can be in the form of an infographic or a scaffolded interactive hyper-slideshow. Coupled with this strategy, teachers can provide different groups of students in your class with a different set of problems by assigning targeted students with a differentiated set of problems. To illustrate this process, there could be an original problem set and then a modified problem set that covers the same concepts. Within the modified problem set, it could be shorter, and it may only have one or two complex multi-step problems versus the original assignment having around ten of these types of problems.

One last area teachers can differentiate online and blended learning math instruction is to provide your students access to adaptive edtech tools like **Khan Academy**, **Freckle**, and **MobyMax**. Using Khan Academy, teachers can assign different groups of students or individual student tutorials and practice problems that relate to areas they need to improve. On MobyMax and Freckle, students can take a pre-assessment where the software can determine what areas need improvement. Then, once the assessment is over, students are given individual tutorials and lessons geared towards what they need to improve. Teachers can track student progress and help along the way to help students in areas they need to improve. Through tracking student progress through this data, teachers can use it to drive their instruction for differentiating other aspects of their math instruction as well as target specific students or groups of students for math interventions.

Conclusion

Chapter 7 provided some insight into how you can differentiate your instruction in online and blended learning educational settings. The goal of this chapter was to provide some basics to help begin differentiating online with the thought that these same strategies can translate back to a face to face classroom.Ultimately, this is only the tip of the iceberg of what teachers can do to differentiate instruction.

Through the use of technology and well-thought-out strategies, there is a multitude of different things teachers can do for their students that can take what we have explained here to the next level. In our future reality of online and blended learning educational settings, differentiation can take place as it did in a face to face classroom setting for synchronous class sessions. Then, adapted and embedded differentiations within edtech tools, as well as targeted differentiation strategies, can be used for online asynchronous instruction.

After reviewing the contents of this chapter, teachers and administrators should consult with their Special Education Ed. Specialist and English Language Coordinator at their school site to work collaboratively to help differentiate instruction for all the students you serve. These conversations should prompt access and action for these specialist teachers to assist you and your students. For example, teachers need to give both of these service and support providers with access to their learning management system. Also, teachers need to email them to consult with them on some of the first decisions you are going to make to differentiate your online and blended learning instruction while designing your course. This will be key as you start to begin slowly with differentiating the instruction of your students. Over time, the goal is to add more differentiation strategies and to add more supports within your instruction and teacher created content as you become more comfortable doing so as your online and blended learning class progresses and evolves as time goes by.

CHAPTER 8

Case Management for Special Education for Online and Blended Learning Settings

Over the spring semester of 2020, we have searched and explored through various Special Education Twitter Chats, Facebook Groups, and resources through the State Department of Education and the U.S. Department of Education, to see how to serve students through an online learning model effectively. It prompted a further look into how to best access students, collect data, collaborate with teachers, provide feedback to students and parents, and to communicate directly with the student and all pertinent service providers. As a result, it allowed for an opportunity to compile several useful edtech tools to help with case managing students enrolled in Special Education in K-12 schools. Ultimately, the goal of this chapter is to help Special Education case managers work with their students on their caseload more effectively in online and blended learning educational settings by incorporating various edtech tools to help facilitate and streamline their case management duties

Before moving on to the contents of this chapter, be aware that every state and district has must follow the laws and policies derived from the Individuals with Disabilities Education Act (IDEA) regarding working with students with special needs. New guidance directives from the United States Department of Education on Special Education related issues on March 13th and June 22nd respond to the challenges presented by the pandemic. From this new guidance, it may change how your school may be moving forward with Special Education programs and services during the toggled term when we are toggling between online and blended learning educational settings (U.S. Department of Education, 2020). Due to these new policy guidelines, districts and schools will have to interpret these guidelines and possibly change practices, if necessary, to ensure students with special needs are receiving a free and appropriate education under IDEA. As a result, keep your district and school's evolving Special Education policies in mind as we discuss the various strategies to make case management a much more effective process for all service providers and stakeholders involved in the student's education. For this chapter, the edtech tools we are going to focus on are located within Google's **G-Suite** since the vast majority of schools and districts have access to these tools.

Communication with Parents and Students - Google Voice

Regardless of the educational setting, communication with Special Education students and their families is key to ensure students are making progress through the curriculum, socio-emotionally, and able to access services and accommodations outlined in their IEPs. Since all teachers are going to be bouncing between their brick and mortar office/classroom phones and their home office, one way to communicate with families and students while conducting remote learning is through **Google Voice**. Google Voice is a free service that allows you to use one phone number in place of your existing phone number. This allows teachers to have a phone on hand with a number not designated to a personal phone, which is essential as teachers never want to use a personal number for work duties.

Google Voice has several key features that can help Special Education teachers communicate with parents and students on their caseload. Google Voice can be accessed on a PC or smartphone, which gives users access to the service anywhere where you have access to the internet. Additionally, there is a feature that allows for all incoming calls using the Google Voice number to be sent directly to your current mobile phone (without your real number being used) to take the call. Also, when voice calls and text messages are sent, they are automatically logged into Google Voice's memory. They can be used as ongoing records of phone calls and texts to ensure accountability and transparency with parents (be aware that teachers need to be sure to let parents and students know that all communications are recorded). As a result, there is a repository of text and call records teachers and administrators can access if there is a need to review.

Google Voice is a great tool that can help Special Education teachers communicate with their students to ensure they are participating in online and blended learning on a daily/weekly basis. Through the use of Google Voice, teachers will be able to streamline communications to contact families to ensure accountability with students as well as assess how they are doing socio-emotionally and academically.

IEP Meetings - Google Meet & Google Calendar

Annual IEP meetings may look much different during an online or blended learning setting. Different states, districts, and schools will have a variety of different methods to adapt instruction to implement IEP services. When school begins in the fall of 2020 and onwards, a toggled term could result in IEP meetings having to be conducted digitally online throughout the school year. Thus, meeting on a safe platform is a must, which means at this point, **Google Meet**, **Zoom**, and **Microsoft Teams** are currently the best widely used platforms to conduct IEP meetings due to their collaborative functions and accessibility.

Google Meet, Zoom, and Microsoft Teams are prominent meeting platforms because they have all of the critical features needed for IEP meetings. They all contain a scheduling apparatus through **Google Calendar** and **Microsoft Outlook** (click more options and then create your Google Meet, Zoom, or Microsoft Teams meeting on each calendar), screen sharing, and video/audio recording. Also, just as important, an active link can be sent to any participant by email; if this is the mechanism teachers would like to send IEP meeting invites to parents and service providers.

Collecting IEP Data - Google Forms and SurveyMonkey

Collecting IEP data remotely for academic goals may have some hurdles, depending on how goals are written. Still, there are many ways to collect ongoing data within an online learning educational setting to help provide evidence students are making progress on IEP goals as well as moving forward with their present levels. **Google Forms** and **SurveyMonkey** are efficient and practical tools to send out present level surveys to a student's general education teachers and pertinent IEP service providers (i.e., Speech Therapist, Psychologist, Physical Therapist, Occupational Therapist, etc.)

In the case of present level surveys, they can be generalized so teachers can provide pertinent teacher input for reading, writing, math, science, communication, executive functioning, vocational, and behavior. Questions on the survey can be open-ended, and in the form of a multiple-choice/Likert scale, it is your choice. While developing the survey, be sure always to provide a demographic section of the form for teachers to provide the student's name, date, and service, class, or subject they cover. Also, remember to create a specific form for each student by writing their name at the top of it to ensure all teachers and service providers know which student they are completing for the present level survey. Finally, to ensure everyone will fill out your survey, the survey should only take no more than 3 to 5 minutes to complete as general education teachers and service providers will have other present level surveys to complete during the week. Ultimately, to make things much more transparent, school sites and districts should develop standardized present level surveys for Special Education teachers at the primary and secondary levels. By having this for an entire district can access and send out, it will ensure general education teachers have a standardized survey they are familiar with to complete for their students.

Concerning goal data collection, **Google Forms** or **SurveyMonkey** can be built specifically with the IEP goals in mind. This will require teachers and service providers to complete the survey by providing evidence of whether students are making progress or not with the curriculum being provided online. Similar to the present level survey, the goal survey needs to have an introductory demographic section for general education teachers and service providers and then have the goal input questions be open-ended so they can input the data. Finally, to be prepared for an upcoming IEP meeting, Special Education teachers need to be sure to send the goal progress surveys out to teachers and service providers via email at least two weeks in advance before the meeting in order to provide enough time to collect the data. Attend to the results of the survey throughout the two weeks leading up to the meeting to ensure everyone has completed it. If a teacher or service provider has not completed the survey, send it out to them again until they complete the survey.

Conclusion

Case management is one of the most challenging parts of the job for Special Education teachers. Through this chapter, teachers and administrators should be able to think about how edtech tools can help with the case management of students. Besides, teachers should feel encouraged to think about other edtech tools they have at their disposal within their district and school to integrate into the case management of their students. At the end of the day, the goal is to be the most effective and efficient with Special Education case management so teachers can serve all of their students to the best of their ability regardless of their educational setting.

CHAPTER 9

IEP Meetings During a Toggled Term - Recommendation for Preparing and Conducting Effective Online IEP Meeting

Beyond case management, being prepared to hold IEP meetings online is critical. For all districts around the country, Special Education will not be temporarily halted this fall semester as it did for some schools this past spring. During the spring, districts and Special Education teachers have scrambled to ensure students are receiving services and supports. As discussed in the previous chapter, annual IEP meetings must be held. To review, annual IEP meetings are where service providers, parents, and all stakeholders in a student's education meet to determine how the student is doing in a variety of different areas as well as determine how to adjust their IEP to facilitate their learning best. Regardless of whether we will be either an online or blended learning environment this fall, there will be federally mandated timelines and procedures that must take place to ensure the IEP meeting is conducted, written, and implemented. Thus, the IEP document is the basis of all K-12 education services in the United States.

Each district school has its own policies regarding IEP meetings that are extremely important to review before holding online IEP meetings. Teachers and administrators alike need to continually check and review district and school policies as they will be evolving much more quickly due to circumstances the next 12 to 18 months will bring. This may be intimidating at first, but we can assure you that the online meetings themselves will be held like any other IEP meeting we would hold in brick and mortar K-12 schools. During this time, asking questions and clarifying policies with Special Education administrators at the district level will be important as changes to policy come out over time. However, in the meantime, we can focus on several areas of best practice that will likely fit around any new changes to preparing and holding IEPs in the future. Ultimately, the goal of this chapter is to provide several critical recommendations on how to prepare for an online IEP meeting in an efficient manner and then outline several tips and tricks for holding a productive online IEP meeting. Lastly, it's also important to note that many of these suggestions will be translatable to IEP meetings that occur in-person once schools begin fully opening and allowing meetings once again on campus.

Tips for Getting Ready for an Online IEP Meeting

Getting ready for IEP meetings is critical to having them be successful for all parties involved. As a result, provided are 11 essential steps to prepare for upcoming meetings. This process involves collecting pertinent data for present levels and goals, organizing key documents, writing the IEP, and scheduling the meeting. As you review each recommendation, think about your current practices or how Special Educations at your school prepares for IEP meetings. Think about all of the steps required to ensure they can occur as a routine before the meeting begins. Finally, think about how your district and school can develop protocols for the future to help Special Education teachers and general education teachers understand best practice preparation procedures to ensure future IEP meetings can be held.

- Ensure you have a Google Drive or folder available for all documents and IEP pages relating to the student. Keep all of the documents in one place to stay organized. Digital organization is vital.

- Utilize Google Forms or SurveyMonkey to develop a survey to ask teachers questions regarding the student's present levels. Include questions relating to each section of the present levels page.

- Use the student information system your school is using to analyze the demographic data, grade book, and transcript of the student to help complete the information page, transition pages, present levels, and goal progress pages.

- Gain access to view student work in their online learning management system being used in their academic classes (i.e., Seesaw, Google Classroom, Schoology, Canvas, etc.). This will allow case managers to gain access to work samples of their students to help with present levels and goal progress.

- Email your student/parents a transition survey (if they are in high school) for them to complete you have information to complete the transition pages of the IEP.

- Draft the majority of the IEP and send out parts of the IEP beforehand for the parent to review (follow your district's rules regarding drafting IEP's before meetings).

- Schedule the meeting at least two weeks in advance, if possible. Use Google Voice, email, or use *67 to call parents/guardians to schedule the meeting.

- Practice connecting with parents with the virtual meeting software, so they know how to use it before the scheduled meeting.

- Invite the student if they are of middle school and high school age. Even though it is an online meeting, they need to be included because it is their IEP to support them.

- Follow up email with pertinent documents. You will be required to send a follow-up email after you have scheduled the IEP on the calendar with pertinent documents and a link or phone number to join the virtual meeting. Do this ahead of time.

- After the meeting is over, send parent the full agreed-upon IEP via email (be sure to review district protocols)

- Be sure to have a signature program available for e-signatures or protocols in place to obtain and document verbal and written consent.

Tips for Conducting an Online IEP Meeting

IEP meetings in the future will likely be held in multiple capacities either online, partially online, or in-person (i.e., parents video conferencing in), and in-person for the next 12 to 18 months. This could mean there could be times when IEP meetings will be held entirely online or partially in-person throughout the semester. In all likelihood, there may be times districts and schools will have to toggle back and forth between having online and in-person meetings. Or, IEP meetings may be held only online indefinitely. Therefore, Special Education teachers, general education teachers, and administrators all need to be involved in understanding how IEP meetings can be held effectively online. As with the recommendations for preparing for an online IEP meeting, think about your current practices as well as your school and district's best practices for holding IEP meetings. How can these current practices be refined for the future? As you review these recommendations, think about how they can be refined to the reality of a toggled term.

- Review district online IEP protocols. Some districts have an IEP meeting script case managers can follow.

- Provide an agenda of the IEP meeting to participants and parents/guardians in separate emails before the meeting begins.

- Provide a start time and end time along with the agenda through the online calendar invite or email sent out before the meeting begins. Also, ensure everyone is on the same page regarding time specifications.

- Be sure to order various meeting participants so they can all provide input. Provide possible time limits to ensure the meeting stays on task and on time.

- Before the meeting begins, the very first question is to ask parents/guardians their main concerns regarding their student's progress. Be prepared for questions about online instruction.

- Case managers should share their screens throughout the virtual meeting to review pages of the IEP with the participants of the meeting. Reviewing the IEP as you go is the best method to ensure transparency.

- Take your time in the event the parent/guardian did not go through the draft IEP that was sent beforehand.

- Ask confirmation questions if you are unsure of the parent/guardians' feelings/perspectives towards proposals in the IEP.

- Have a notes template that is flexible. Include the IEP meeting agenda as it will be much easier to fill out during and after the meeting.

- At the end of the meeting, be sure everyone on the IEP team is aware of the consent process (whether it is through e-signatures of another process outlined by district protocols).

Conclusion

At the end of the day, we want IEPs regardless of the education setting to be as smooth as possible. It can be a stressful time for families and teachers because of the transition to online learning and the significant adaptations taking place in Special Education. Also, this transition will continue over time as schools' transition to blended learning and then to full face to face instruction over the next year. As a result, Special Education will have several significant transitions students, teachers, and families who will have to endure, which will cause adaptations to be utilized for each change made in the educational setting. Therefore, teachers and administrators need to focus on making the IEP process as streamlined as much as possible so they can make it easy and efficient for all parties involved. Also, as the situation continues to evolve, Special Educators and administrators need to be highly aware that every district is different and to read thoroughly through the district's online and blended learning IEP procedures. Ask questions, if necessary, on the procedures, even if it is just for clarification. Hopefully, by following the recommendations provided in this chapter, it can build a framework for preparing as well as holding successful IEP meetings for our students. Ultimately, through this success, healthy relationships between the family, student, and IEP service providers can be cultivated, which will lead to positive outcomes for the student and IEP team.

Part 2. Conclusion

Within the next 12 to 18 months, there will be incredible transformations in our education system. Therefore, districts, schools, administrators, and teachers in K-12 education will need to have an idea on how to serve best our students that need us the most during this time. Regardless of whether a teacher is teaching kindergarten, Special Education, or high school English, having an idea of how to engage and communicate with students online, differentiate instruction using edtech for online and blended learning settings, and being knowledgeable about Special Education case management and the IEP meeting process, is critical for schools to navigate and toggle between online learning and blended learning educational settings successfully.

Ultimately, each educator within the school community will have to have this foundational understanding of specialized areas for districts and schools to toggle back and forth between online and blended learning successfully. Think about the following scenario. There will be weeks and possibly even months of a blended learning educational setting, and then suddenly, it could shift directly back to full online instruction for days, weeks, or even months. Thus, toggling between various educational settings may be an often occurrence. Therefore, how can we transition back and forth without knowledge about how all school business is conducted online and face to face? The simple answer is that we need to know how to conduct all functions of a school in both online and blended learning settings seamlessly and simultaneously so student learning can be continuous.

As we progress forward to Part 3, we will see what all districts, schools, administrators, and teachers need to evaluate before developing and solidifying plans for the fall and beyond. We will need to assess future scenarios of what online and blended learning environments will look like, as well as incorporating new procedures to ensure the health and safety of our students and teachers. Part 3 is designed to help answer questions about how we can accommodate all of our students and teachers on campus with social distance and hygiene protocols in place. Further, Part 3 will address the best practices of blended learning and what it looks like in practice. Then, it will focus on how teachers can continue their professional learning to put themselves in the best position possible to create innovative solutions for their students. Additionally, our focus will be on how teachers can use social networks as the professional learning community to collaboratively build capacity to solve the challenges our districts and schools will face as we continue to navigate this crisis.

PART 3

Navigating Fall 2020 and Beyond, Reopening Schools, Learning Models that can Toggle, and Continued Professional Development

With foundational knowledge and background in several niche areas in education that will undergo significant changes due to the realities of the future realities of a toggled term, conversations can begin about developing plans to reopen schools in the fall. Regardless of where a district or school is located, many of the same priorities will need to be assessed to ensure students, teachers, and staff will be safe to reenter schools initially and then prepare for the long-term. Alluded throughout Part 1 and Part 2, social distancing and hyper hygienic protocols will need to be in place, which will reshape how students and teachers interact with school facilities and each other going forward. As a result, this will affect instructional models because, in many cases, schools will not be able to have all of their students on campus at a time. Simply put, it will be too dangerous to do this at first and secondary schools will have to evolve and plan for this going forward.

Part 3 will be dedicated to discussing how districts and schools can have conversations with teachers, parents, students, and health authorities about initially reopening in some capacity in the future and navigating the next 12 to 18 months. First, within Chapter 10, a number of priorities will be outlined for districts and schools to assess before developing plans to reopen. Also, this discussion will include which populations of student's schools should first open their doors too. Then, the conversation will shift towards staggered scheduling to accommodate social distancingand hygiene protocols by providing scenarios for primary and secondary schools to consider. To build onto the discussion of reopening schools, Chapter 11 will elaborate on blended learning as an instructional model that can be implemented with staggered scheduling. Several blended learning models will be discussed as well as best practices associated with the blended learning will be expanded upon throughout Chapter 11. To build upon the blended learning models outlined in Chapter 11, Chapter 12 will provide an instructional model to ensure learning is continuous at secondary schools regardless of the circumstances. Also, this instructional model will take into consideration the choices parents make in light of the instructional options given to them when schools initially reopen. Finally, for teachers and administrators to put themselves in the best position to problem solve when challenges arise as a result of the realities a toggled term presents, Chapter 13 will focus on cultivating ongoing professional development. Professional development in this context will expand on the notion of sharing and consuming ideas with the worldwide educational community. To meet this end, educators will learn about the innovator's mindset as a philosophy to build their own professional brand to share their expertise with others and to develop professional learning networks to be in the position to build capacity continuously as an educator to meet the demands and challenges presented by the toggled term.

By evaluating how schools will initially reopen, outlining the instructional models that will be available to use in this ongoing scenario of navigating the toggled term, and how to develop as an educator further professionally will put educators in secondary schools in a strong position to navigate the fall and beyond. It will help districts and schools throughout the United States prepare and be ready to offer innovative solutions to our future realities presented by this pandemic. The toggled term will not be an easy challenge to overcome for K-12 education. Those who are not prepared will be struck hard by these challenges. Lives are at stake. But, there's hope. By having a pragmatic and planned approach alongside an innovator's mindset, secondary educators will be ready to initially reopen schools to ease back face to face instruction through blended learning with the ability to transition back to full online instruction continuously.

CHAPTER 10

The Initial Reopening of K-12 Schools in the Fall of 2020 - Priorities to Assess, Students with Special Needs, and Staggered Schedules

During the spring of 2020, numerous articles are being produced by states and local county offices of education regarding recommendations to initially reopen schools next fall (Centers for Disease Control, 2020; California Department of Education, 2020; San Diego County of Education, 2020). As we evaluate the recommendations for the ongoing reopening of society and the economy proposed by the federal and state governments, we learned it would be in phases with schools being part of the equation. Based on the step by step process of opening the economy, schools are the vital element in doing so successfully. Thus, districts and schools throughout the nation will need to plan for the fall semester continuously and beyond because the COVID-19 crisis will likely last another 12 to 18 months based on estimations by medical researchers for the development of a vaccine and treatments for the disease (Time, 2020). As a result, schools will not be returning to 'normal' upon the return to school in the fall. Thus, proactively planning will allow schools to initially re-open this fall in an effective manner where students will be receiving quality instruction as well as in a safe learning environment that can adapt to changes in the number of local COVID-19 cases.

Now, there will be a conversation describing several priorities district and school leaders need to consider while developing short term plans to initially reopen and long-term plans to navigate the toggled term. Secondly, part of the conversation will briefly touch on which populations of student's schools should consider in the initial reopening and how to support them as school's toggle between some form of face to face learning and online learning. Then, there will be a discussion on staggered schedules for secondary schools and the options that leaders could consider when developing their plans to reopen this fall. After the conversation on staggered schedules, the cohort model will also be touched on as a viable model for the challenges presented by the size of large secondary schools.

First Priorities to Assess Before Developing a Plan to Reopen in the Fall

After evaluating several vital articles and recommendations produced by the Centers for Disease Control (2020), California Department of Education (2020), and the San Diego County of Education (2020), a list of priorities has been compiled for secondary school and district leaders and teachers to consider while planning to initially reopen schools as well as their long-term plans to navigate the toggled term. Be aware that there is no specific order to any of these priorities. Still, they all must be considered for developing plans to initially reopen schools and long-term plans for any type of face to face instruction for the fall and beyond.

- Assess on an on-going basis how distance learning is going with teachers, students, and parents. What were the areas of success and improvement? Evaluate through online instruction climate surveys to all parties, administrator observations of online synchronous and asynchronous instruction, and student participation data in each form of online instruction.

- Communicate with the County Office of Education and collaborate with the County Health Office to determine what procedures and protocols need to be included in district/ school reopening plans.

- Conduct a student, staff, and facility safety assessment. Assess how social distancing protocols and procedures provided by the state could affect the campus on a short term and long-term basis by evaluating school facilities and student enrollment.

- Evaluate how social distancing could affect daily instructional schedules, passing periods, lunch, recess, PE, and entering/exiting campus by students and staff.

- Assess students that are considered at-risk (Foster Youth, ELL, and low SES), students with disabilities, and students who did not participate in distance learning. Consult with the county and state regarding IEPs and how a blended learning or distance learning model may alter Special Education Services going forward

- Research blended learning and distance learning instructional models as well as schools that have reopened with social distancing protocols and altered instructional models. Currently, we see schools beginning to re-open around the world. We can also look to see how China, Thailand, Israel, Canada, and several European countries (i.e., Denmark, Austria, etc.) who have reopened their public schools to determine if any protocols they employed in their schools can also be used in our schools. During this process, leaders need to assess what has been working thus far for schools that have reopened.

- Collaborate with teachers and local teacher associations for assessing each of these priorities on how to support them best as schools reopen as well as in the development of the reopening plan.

- Collaborate with local, state, and federal educational authorities on funding, logistics, and recommendations/ guidelines for re-opening schools.

Use School Openings to Help Students Who Are Most At-Risk and Students with Disabilities

Schools and districts need to take students who are most at risk and students with disabilities into account when thinking about moving back to brick and mortar education settings and the long-term implications of this move. Leaders need to assess which students may be most at-risk for infection. Additionally, leaders need to assess how students more at-risk and with disabilities can attend the school facilities. For students with moderate/severe disabilities, which are not related to health (i.e., health fragility to any infection), the brick and mortar school buildings could be the best option for these students as they need additional resources and services. Typically, the numbers of these students' schools serve are low, which would allow for classrooms to have less than 12 students, an ideal environment for Specialized Academic Instruction and social distancing protocols to be simultaneously implemented.By using the actual school facility for students with the highest needs, it can accommodate their learning needs first and foremost. Then, it can provide Special Education teachers the opportunity not to have to reinvent their IEP as the services in place from the previous school year would be similar to what they were before the crisis began.

Schools should consider first opening their doors to these student populations as they are the most at-need for the services and support schools provided by Special Education teachers. By providing these students with in-person instruction, it will help the most vulnerable, and the most at need have instruction, which will allow facilities to be once again occupied by students and teachers.

Staggered Days and Schedules with Social Distancing Protocols

In order to initially reopen schools and have some form of in-person instruction, there will need to be some form of staggered scheduling to occur to ensure social distancing protocols can be implemented. Many proposals regarding staggering school days and schedules will help with implementing social distance policies. Ultimately, this would look different in primary and secondary schools, but, in theory, weeks would look like 20% to 50% of the student population attending school one to three days per week. Additionally, school days could also be cut in half where one group of students attends in the morning while the other group of students attends in the afternoon. As stated above, this will depend on a variety of different variables in play. The variables that need to be taken into consideration whether this is a viable option for specific school sites includes the following: 1) student population (larger schools like high schools will have a much more difficult time to implement staggered days versus small elementary schools), 2) facility layout, how logistically the staggered schedules would be arranged (logistically, secondary class schedules will be much more difficult for staggered days), 3) integrating social distancing protocols into every single aspect of the school's functions (i.e., instructional settings, hallways, PE, entrances/exits, lunchroom, etc.) and, most importantly, student and teacher safety. Leaders need to take into consideration these variables as they are essential in assessing whether staggering schedules is the best option for initially reopening schools and navigating the toggled term on a long-term basis. Overall, at the end of the day, this decision-making process has been given to local school districts to make so they can best support their students and local communities. Therefore, there will be incredible diversity as to how instruction will be scheduled.

Below, there are several scenarios provided that illustrate how staggered schedules could be implemented for secondary schools for the fall semester and beyond. Overall, for secondary schools, there are three options to consider and evaluate that seem plausible to implement beginning in the fall, and over the next 12 to 18 months. Additionally, the cohort model will also be examined as an option to restrict the total number of students interact with on a daily or weekly basis. Within each scenario, there are several pros and cons to consider that are associated with each staggered schedule option secondary schools should consider for their initial reopening and long-term plans.

Secondary Staggered Schedule Options

Option 1: A secondary school could implement a one-day in-person face to face class day for its by dividing the school population into 25% segments that would take up the days of Monday-Thursday (i.e., Group A, B, C, and D). During this day, 25% of the population at the school site would complete a standard 5 to 7 period where students receive face to face instruction. Generally, during these days, it would provide teachers and students time to connect for small group instruction as well as to receive time for in-person activities. Then, the remainder of the week, students would have supplemental online instruction.

Pros: Lower Probability of Contact with Others, Higher Student and Teacher Safety Due to Smaller Groups on Campus, and Social Distancing Friendly

Cons: Low Amount of Face to Face Instruction and Predominantly Online Instruction

In this option, students receive one day face to face instruction a week but have the majority of instruction online. However, students and teachers receive the least exposure to others. Additionally, this could provide large schools an option outside of alternating weeks of face to face instruction for their students like outlined in Option 3. For example, a school of 3000+ students would equate to about 750 students per day on campus, which would allow for social distance protocols to be adequately followed when staggered schedules are implemented for arrival, dismissal, and between class periods.

Option 2: A secondary school could implement an even and odd day block schedule for two face to face days per week. In this model, upwards to 50% of the school population would attend odd and even days on Monday-Thursday. During these odd and even day block periods, students would receive longer instructional times with their teachers and peers for in-person activities. Then, on days students are not attending school; online instruction would supplement what they are learning in class.

Pros: High Amounts of Face to Face Instruction and Minimal Online Instruction

Cons: Higher Probability of Contact with Others, Lower Amounts of Student and Teacher Safety Due to Large Groups on Campus, Not Social Distance Friendly

In this option, secondary schools would have to ensure they could institute social distancing policies, with 50% of students present at the school site. Instructional face to face time would be equal to Option 3, but there would be more students present in classes. Ultimately, this could be a viable plan if the secondary school has a smaller student population of fewer than 1200 students. It would allow students in these scenarios to adequately socially distance and receive more face to face instruction. However, for larger schools, this option may not be viable as 50% of students of a school of 3000+ would equate to almost 1500 students on campus, which would likely not be doable with social distance protocols.

Option 3: A secondary could implement rotation weeks of face to face and online instruction for different groups of students. There would be four groups of students, amounting to 25% of the student population for each group. Then, two groups per week would go to school in person while the other two groups work online for the week. For example, during the first week of the month, group A would attend periods one through six on Monday and Wednesday. Then, group B could attend periods one through six on Tuesday and Thursday. The following week, groups C and D would attend in-person, while groups A and B would be receiving online instruction.

Pros: High Amount of Face to Face Instruction, Lower Probability of Contact with Others, Higher Student and Teacher Safety Due to Smaller Groups on Campus, and Social Distancing Friendly

Cons: Face to Face Instructional Time Split in Half with Online Instruction

For this option of instruction, students would receive longer times of face to face instruction in addition to not being around large groups of students. Teachers would also be around a smaller number of students daily. However, with this weekly rotating schedule, there ultimately would be less face to face time for students, but almost equal to the number of face to face instruction as Option 1. For large schools with populations of students 3000+, it could be a viable option as 25% of the students would equate to fewer than 750 students at the school site. To this end, it would make it much easier to institute social distancing protocols and ensure student safety at large school sites.

The Cohort Model

The cohort model could be another option that involves the staggering of schedules. Based on the Center for Disease Control (2020) May 2020 Report, it provided recommendations to schools regarding reopening in the future, which opened the doors to the viability of the cohort model being implemented in secondary schools. One of the most significant takeaways from the report discussed significantly restricting student to student contact and any intermingling with groups of students on campus. What this means is that passing times between classes may be challenging to implement. Staggered bells could be a possibility to alleviate contact while passing periods occur. But this is not ideal unless the secondary school utilizes **Option 1** of the staggered schedules presented because it only allows for 25% of the student body to be on campus at a single moment.

One model that should be given consideration is the cohort model. Cohorts are made up of one continuous body of students that go from class to class together from the beginning to the end of the school day. Instead of moving from one class to another, students will stay in a single classroom while on campus. To ensure students do not make any contact with students from outside their cohort, teachers could move from one classroom to another class throughout the day instead of students. For larger secondary schools, the cohort model may be much more challenging to implement because of the logistics involved. For example, the hurdles could include the logistics of creating the student cohorts, developing a master schedule for the rotation of teachers, and figuring out how to fit students who do not need certain classes into specific cohort groups who have some of the classes still required for them to advance to high school from middle school or to fulfill graduation requirements for high school. However, once some of these initial hurdles are overcome, cohorts could likely have more than double face to face instructional time as outlined in Option 1, 2, and 3 of the proposed staggered schedules. Since students are not moving throughout the day on the physical campus, the major logistical challenge of restricting contact and intermingling of students outside of the cohort would be entering and exiting the school before and after school.

Pros: High Amounts of Face to Face Instructional Time, Lower Probability of Contact with Others, Higher Student and Teacher Safety Due to Smaller Groups on Campus, and Social Distancing Friendly

Cons: Logistical and Scheduling Nightmare for Large Secondary Schools

The cohort model is a viable model going forward for secondary schools. The smaller the secondary school, the simpler and more accessible the cohort model will be to implement. The larger the secondary school, the more complex the cohort model is to implement. For the amount of instruction and lower probably of contact with other students, it is a scheduling and grouping model that should be considered for some schools when they are considering to reopen in the fall and beyond.

Conclusion

More than likely, student scheduling staggering options for primary and secondary school will comprise the elements outlined in the priorities and scenarios presented in this chapter. The initial priorities provided earlier in the chapter should be reviewed, assessed, and then developed into a plan before a school and district decide on how they should stagger student schedules to lower the probability of possible COVID-19 infection for both students and teachers.

Within these plans, we must further reiterate that schools and districts need to prepare for the "toggled" term. The probability of closing a school down short term will be high. Thus, staggered scheduling offered in secondary schools will need to be able to toggle to fully online instruction at a moment's notice if a COVID-19 case occurs on a school campus. Or, the number of cases increases within the school and district's jurisdiction that make it unsafe to attend school. As a result, both scenarios depict why districts and secondary schools must be prepared to offer a blended instructional model that has been consistently alluded to and reiterated throughout this book. It allows for the flexibility to transition, in the form of a toggle, immediately to online instruction to allow for continuous learning to occur with a stoppage.

CHAPTER 11

Blended Learning is the Future - Types of Blended Learning Models for Fall 2020 and Beyond

As we continue to think about the fall semester and beyond, blended learning models appear to be one of the most viable options on the table for when schools reopen. As discussed in the previous chapter, recommendations from the federal government, states, and local county offices of education provided that there will be a time where schools will ease back into face to face instruction over the course of the school year utilizing a hybrid model and providing alternative online options to any form of in-person instruction. During this period, schools and districts will introduce social distancing protocols, staggering schedules, and continuing some form of online learning as options for families to consider for the school year. More than likely, face to face instruction will be limited at first as the reopening of schools occurs. Likely, face to face instruction may only be a couple of days per week, to begin with, and then it may open up further if the number of COVID-19 cases declines within the local county over time.

Additionally, new treatments for the disease may also affect future decisions regarding adding more days of face to face instruction. Thus, in all likelihood, when taking into account all of the recommendations by the federal, state, and local education and health authorities, when schools reopen this fall and beyond, it will be a combination of face to face and online learning educational settings. The name of this form of this hybrid instruction is called blended learning. Blended learning will ultimately allow for flexible educational settings that will allow schools to toggle back and forth between face to face and online instruction.

Blended learning is what we would call an integration between face to face and online learning experiences (Ferdig & Kennedy, 2018). In a sense, both types of educational settings are synthesized together to create an educational setting that can be implemented in-person and online simultaneously. Ultimately, blended learning has a variety of different definitions, as several different models can be used to implement blended learning. Thus, the goal of this chapter is to outline various blended learning models as well as provide secondary teachers and administrators with blended learning best practices. To round out this chapter, there will be a short discussion on how to incorporate student engagement strategies into a blended learning face to face and online synchronous live sessions. By the end of this chapter, teachers and administrators will be armed with foundational knowledge on how blended learning works and how it can be practically implemented into K-12 schools as a viable instructional model for the fall of 2020 and beyond.

Blended Learning Models

There is a continuum of blended learning models that can be considered by teachers and administrators when thinking about how to implement blended learning models in K-12 schools. To illustrate the types of blended learning models that are available, there are blended learning models at each end of the spectrum of what blended learning has to offer that have differing amounts of online and face to face instruction. The blended learning models we want to look at are the models that provide required face to face and online components that are simultaneously blended. Additionally, these blended learning models should also fit staggered scheduling and cohort options for secondary settings as a result of the implementation of social distancing and safety protocols in schools.

Secondary Blended Learning

Secondary blended learning could take shape by having students attend school one to three times a week and have the remaining portion of the class online. This could also look like students attending in the morning or afternoon for face to face sessions and have the remainder of the class have an online component. Either way, the staggered scheduling for students to have face to face time will dictate the amount of face to face vs. online instructional time students will have. In all likelihood, the flipped classroom model of blended learning will be utilized for both primary and secondary classes the most often due to its flexibility, which is why we are going to cover this model of blended learning the most in-depth. With this said, the flipped classroom model will be implemented and utilized for secondary settings. Lastly, a short discussion of the Inside-Out and Flex models of blended learning will round out this discussion.

The Flipped Classroom Model. The flipped classroom model of blended learning is a combination of online and face to face synchronous class sessions and asynchronous instruction (Synder et al., 2014). The flipped classroom model can be utilized in two-ways for blended learning. First, it can mean the content and skills students are taught can be frontloaded either online asynchronously or in the face to face synchronous sessions. Ultimately, this is predicated on whether instructional leaders believe students are best suited to take in content and skills online or face to face first. For the face to face component of the flipped classroom model, it could provide opportunities for small group and one on one instruction for students. When content is frontloaded, online students can receive additional support and tutorials in class to practice the content and skills they are taught initially online (Tucker, 2012). Teachers can provide feedback to students in person, and students can be given opportunities to demonstrate their learning with an in-person assessment. Conversely, another possible avenue is frontloading the content during the face to face sessions and then providing students opportunities to practice and demonstrate their learning online through assessment. Thus, teachers would provide much of their feedback online and then re-teach content during subsequent face to face sessions.

For the online component of the flipped classroom model, content, activities/assignments, and assessments can be developed using a module-like style to organize what students need to complete chronologically in an asynchronous manner before a class meets in-person. Teachers need to ensure they can organize their learning management system (i.e., in modules, themes, units, etc.) in a way that can allow students to see their progression in the content, tasks, activities, assignments, and assessments they are asked to complete as they move through the coursework (Tucker, 2012). What this sequence allows students to see is what is due and what is needed to be done before face to face synchronous sessions. For a content-heavy asynchronous online component of a flipped classroom, it could include watching several lectures while taking notes that would ultimately prepare students for a face to face Socratic seminar. On the other hand, for an asynchronous online component of a flipped classroom, it could include several scaffolded assignments before students are given an online assessment on the content and skills they were taught. These tasks could be before having a culminating activity in the synchronous face to face session to demonstrate their learning further by putting it into practice when students meet in in-person with their teacher.

One additional area to consider for the flipped classroom blended learning model, elements of project-based learning can be incorporated into this model. This will allow students to collaborate with their peers and teachers online and in-person to develop creative student work projects to demonstrate their learning. By incorporating project-based learning to the flipped classroom model, an entire district, school, or individual teachers have the option to utilize it depending on how they would like to assess their students' learning and engage their student population.

Flipped Classroom – Online vs. Face to Face Components	
Online Component	**Face to Face Component**
• Asynchronous • Frontloading content (readings, videos, notes) • Content modules online with lectures and tutorials • Assignments, projects, and assessments online • Online office hours available	• Synchronous • Group discussions, Socratic seminars, centers/stations, and student collaboration in-person • One on one tutorials, guided instruction, and in-person feedback • Assignments, projects, and assessments • In-person office hours

Figure 11.1. Flipped Classroom – Online vs. Face to Face Components

Other Blended Learning Options. Beyond the flipped classroom model, several other blended learning models must also be mentioned. First, the Inside-Out Model is another form of blended learning secondary educators can consider. For the Inside-Out Model as outlined by Ferdig and Kennedy (2018), students begin classes face to face (on one single day or it could be extended to a week-long) and then complete the vast majority of the coursework online. Then, by the last day or week of the class, there will be a culminating face to face class students would attend (Ferdig & Kennedy, 2018). This model is generally used at the graduate school level, but the likelihood this model could be used in K-12 seems unlikely because it is too great of a distance between face to face class sessions. Realistically, the plausibility of this model being used is little; but, for Advanced Placement classes at the high school, it could be a possibility to consider.

The second additional blended learning model that can be considered much more widely in K-12 is the Flex Blended Learning Model. In this blended learning model, a subject or course is based primarily online, and students can complete it at their own pace (Ferdig & Kennedy, 2018). Throughout the semester, students check in weekly with the teacher of record at the school site to assess their progress. Students also can schedule their personalized one on one tutorials with their teacher. The Flex Blended Learning Model can arguably be considered what personalized learning looks like because students and families are working at their own pace and utilizing support from a teacher when needed and receiving personalized instruction when they meet synchronously for tutorials. Ultimately, what this looks like is a flexible model for face to face instructional support for students if social distancing protocols only allow for a small percentage of students on campus at a time. Currently, many high school independent study and K-12 homeschooling programs utilize this model of learning for their blended learning model. Thus, due to the widespread use of this model, it could be a plausible choice for many secondary schools to adopt that want to ease back in face to face learning overtime as well as have the ability to toggle back to fully online instruction if needed quickly and seamlessly.

Blended Learning Models		
Flipped Classroom	**Inside-and-Out**	**Flex**
• Asynchronous frontloaded content online (i.e., lectures, modules, notes, etc.) before in-person synchronous sessions. • In-person synchronous sessions on a weekly basis • Assignments and assessments are completed online and in-person	• Primarily asynchronous online instruction • In-person synchronous sessions occur at the beginning of the course and at the end of the course • Online live synchronous sessions occur once or twice a week • Assignments and assessments are completed online and in-person	• Students complete at their own pace • Primarily online • Face to face sessions are optional • Traditionally used for Independent Study courses or homeschooling • Assignments and assessments are done all online

Figure 11. 2. Blend Learning Models

Blended Learning Best Practices

To make blended learning a viable option to navigate the challenges presented by a toggled term, secondary teachers need to be trained in how to utilize this type of learning model going forward. Teachers will need to be trained in both the technical and pedagogical components of blended learning for it to be a successful form of instruction (Tucker, 2016). Through following these two components, teachers need to be aware of several best practice strategies to ensure their blended learning classroom culture flourishes.

For the pedagogical component, teachers need to work on instructional strategies that can be used during small groups, and in one on one instruction. Small group instruction could include elements of student collaboration, activities to find/solve problems, social-emotional learning, critical thinking, and student discussion. One on one instruction could include ways to provide formative and summative feedback, social-emotional learning, goal setting, organization/time management, and direct instruction tutorials for students. Similarly, as with the technical component required for blended learning, teachers already know many of the vital instructional components that can be implemented for their blended learning classrooms.

Best Practices. Beyond the technical and pedagogical components for blended learning, several best practices must be employed to ensure classroom cultures are cultivated and expectations are set at the beginning of the course. Ferdig and Kennedy (2018), Tucker (2016), and Margolis, Porter, and Pitterle (2017) provide recommendations that teachers should be aware of when developing their blended learning classrooms. Below is a list of best practices that teachers need to be sure to develop and then implement in any form of blended learning that is utilized when schools initially reopen as well as for however long social distancing and hyper hygienic practices are required. Additionally, be aware that these recommended practices can also be implemented in full-time face to face classroom settings as well. As a result, once schools return to normal once the pandemic is over, the best practices from blended learning will be engrained in all classroom settings and could become a widely used instructional model in secondary schools we move into the post-COVID-19 world in education.

- **Setting the Stage** - Set expectations on the first day of class. Discuss the structure of the course, technical components, essential dates, and grading information.

- **Consistency with Teaching** - This includes communicating with students through the same medium. Teachers should only communicate with their students through one or two mediums (i.e., through email or directly through the learning management system).

- **Timeliness** - Teachers need to be sure all material is posted on time. Minimally, all materials should be posted two weeks before the assignments due date.

- **Accountability** - Provide credit for the majority of tasks conducted for the course (completion points, assignment points, assessment points, etc.).

- **Structure Active Learning** - Provide engaging lessons during face to face class sessions that include active learning by students.

- **Teacher Feedback on Student Preparation** - Teachers should provide feedback for online learning assignments that lead up to the face to face class session. This includes both formative and summative feedback.

- **Incorporate Student Feedback** - Teachers should provide mechanisms online and face to face settings to include student feedback during the course.

- **Continue Reviewing Online and Face to Face Material Throughout the Class** - Provide tutorials of how to interact with the online and face to face material. Review previous topics that connect to future topics.

- **Technology** - Be sure to choose technology that allows students and teachers a level of flexibility.

- **Utilize Digital/Physical Station Rotations** - Within a blended classroom, stations online and offline can be utilized for student collaboration and scaffolding of student tasks.

Overall, secondary administrators and teachers need to develop blended learning instructional models collaboratively with the technical and pedagogical components and best practices in mind. There must be buy-in from both sides to ensure institutional coherence and transparency is established before blended learning is fully implemented (Fullan, 2010). Also, what we must remember beyond the blended learning model is that structural components within the school system will have to be completely revisited. For example, school systems will have to be able to ensure staggered schedules, social distancing, and hyper hygienic protocols can be enacted if the face to face component of blended learning is implemented in the fall or beyond.

Engagement Strategies for Blended Learning - Face to Face and Online Sessions

Engaging students in any learning model is vital. Luckily, for blended learning, the online and face to face components can provide teachers options to make their class engaging in multiple settings. Many of the following suggestions for student engagement can intermix with both online and face to face class settings. Take a look at the following list of strategies to heighten student engagement. Many of these engagement strategies relate to John Hattie's (2012) findings on the 252 influences and effect sizes related to student achievement as well as George Couro's (2015) work on teaching students to be engaged as innovative learners.

- Class Public Opinion Polls
- Interactive Slides - Pear Deck, Google Slides, Poll Anywhere

- Student Collaboration Tools - G-Suite, Microsoft 365, Online Backchannels, Online Whiteboards, etc.
- Twitter Chats
- Flipgrid and Online Discussion Boards
- Class Brainstorms
- Class Instagram
- Students Assess Peers
- Socratic Seminars
- Individual/Class Project Presentation
- Student Self-Assessment
- Social-Emotional Learning Check-ins
- Class Made Videos Demonstrating Learning
- Student-Choice Projects
- The Use of Backchannels for Classroom Discussions
- Project-Based Learning

At the end of the day, the list of engagement strategies for blended learning can go on and on, which allows teachers to be creative in these educational settings. Furthermore, there are many creative solutions teachers can utilize to allow students to engage and participate in the online and face to face components of blended learning. Teachers will continue to think of outside the box solutions as blended learning becomes the mainstream instructional model for the foreseeable future. Thus, as described in Chapter 13, teachers will need to have an innovative mindset going forward to expand their knowledge and knowhow by relying on their colleagues to refine their practices further. Ultimately, blended learning will be an opportunity to experiment and innovate with as it will be a new instructional model for many secondary teachers.

Conclusion

Blended learning is the future for the next 12 to 18 months. To accommodate social distancing, safety, and hygiene guidelines that will be required for school sites to reopen in some capacity for face to face instruction, there does not seem to be a model that can accommodate these requirements. The blended learning model seems to be the only instructional model available unless the school chooses to remain fully online. Remaining fully online does not seem plausible as the only instructional option offered as the public and government wants schools to initially reopen in some capacity as it will help with the ongoing efforts to grow economy and put Americans back to work. Thus, to ease the initial reopening of schools and to navigate the toggled term, blended learning seems to be the way to go as it can be implemented with staggered scheduling to accommodate social distancing and hygiene guidelines. Additionally, it is an instructional model that can toggle between being entirely online for a period of time if the number of COVID-19 cases increases to a level that is dangerous for students and teachers. Ultimately, if blended learning is mildly successful at a large scale, it may plant the seeds for change in K-12 education going forward because it will create flexibility among teachers and students in addition to personalizing learning for our students.

CHAPTER 12

A Learning Model that can Toggle – A Model for Simultaneous and Continuous Online, Blended, and In-Person Learning

When thinking about the future of instruction, educators, regardless of their grade level, need to think of learning as fluid and happening twenty-four seven. What this means is that students should have access to all of the learning materials and content outside of the traditional classroom setting. We live in a world where this an absolute possibility, so modern classrooms need to reflect this opportunity. With this same logic, we can create instructional models that are blended in how they are manifested and implemented. We can go even further and create flexible instructional models that can seamlessly toggle continuously between online, blended online and in-person learning, and traditional in-person learning simultaneously. How would this instructional model be successful, given our current circumstances?

A future instructional model that can toggle back and forth between a fully online instructional model and a blended learning instructional model is best represented by breaking it down into multiple components. Research on instructional models that intertwine blended and online learning elements align with this thought process as we need to develop instruction within our secondary courses that provide multiple means of representation, action/expression, and engagement (Smith, 2016). What this means is to provide multiple modalities of learning for students to interact with the content presented by their teachers, which is represented by the instructional model utilized. Thus, the purpose of this chapter is to show this in action by demonstrating how asynchronous online instruction and synchronous in-person/online instruction can all occur continuously, simultaneously, and allow for seamless toggles between online and in-person synchronous educational settings.

The Toggled Term Instructional Model

To begin, in order to be inclusive to all students at the secondary level, all instruction and content must be centralized online on a learning management system. Then, from our online learning management systems, all instruction and content can be delivered through asynchronous instruction and synchronous live instruction (i.e., in the form of live class sessions) either online or in-person. For the synchronous class sessions, there will be an option of whether it will occur online, in-person, or in both educational settings simultaneously. Ultimately, the educational setting of the synchronous sessions will depend on local health conditions but can be flexible and switch seamlessly between online and in-person educational settings when needed.

The last element that can be added into this instructional equation is the HyFlex instructional model, which seamlessly allows students to participate in the live synchronous class sessions regardless of whether they are online or at the physical campus in-person (Beatty, 2019). In essence, the HyFlex model provides an avenue for teachers to create content, tasks, assignments, and assessments students can complete instead of attending the synchronous sessions if they cannot physically. Furthermore, when the HyFlex model is incorporated into blended learning, it means students can either attend synchronous sessions digitally while the in-person session is happening or complete an alternative asynchronous task, assignment, or assessment in place of attending the class (Beatty, 2019). Overall, the Hyflex model ties the entire model together because the design of the courses with this a synchronous, asynchronous, and HyFlex component allows for effective learning experiences for students who participate fully online or in a blended online and in-person setting (Beatty, 2019). By putting all of these elements together, it creates the Toggled Term Instructional Model.

Ultimately, these mechanisms outlined the Toggled Term Instructional Model provide instruction to all students to learn anywhere and at any time during a toggled term and gives flexibility to teachers to design their courses. While we hope the health conditions will allow for secondary students to attend school in-person as many days possible as it is deemed safe, there will be times when schools must close down their brick and mortar facilities due to COVID-19 cases. In addition, there will be families who do not want their students to attend any blended in-person classes until a vaccine or further treatments are available for COVID-19. Therefore, secondary classes can be designed with these challenges in mind so that the instructional model developed and employed in schools can represent all students. With an instructional model that can toggle and allow for online and blended in-person learning to occur simultaneously and continuously, it will allow all students to participate and engage in learning. It will also allow teachers to have a framework in place where they can successfully deliver their instruction in a manageable and flexible manner to all of their students without interruption.

The Toggled Term Instructional Model for Secondary Schools in Action

Now, it is time to see the Toggled Term Instructional Model in action. Figure 12.1 provides an outline of what this instructional model looks like, as well as how it functions. First, at the top of Figure 12.1, we have asynchronous instruction as the overarching instruction model taking place regardless of whether secondary schools have in-person sessions or are in situations where they have to be entirely online. As we can see, asynchronous instruction takes many forms and provides students with ample opportunities to learn at their own pace. When designing courses, teachers need to ensure asynchronous online instruction is the centerpiece of all the instruction they provide. This entails all course materials/content, class routines, tasks, assignments, and assessments that are derived from their asynchronous instruction. As a result, when instruction is initially originating from asynchronous instruction, it allows for flexibility for synchronous instruction as well as provides equity to students to have full access to the course regardless of the local health conditions.

For synchronous instruction, depending on the local health conditions, instruction can take the form of live synchronous class sessions either in online or in-person educational settings scheduled on specific times and days throughout the week. During live synchronous instruction sessions, many of the same instructional strategies can be implemented to help students engage in the content and skills being taught. However, it must be noted that the instructional strategies for the live online synchronous sessions may require more edtech tools to be in place to manifest the instructional strategies that can be implemented during in-person class sessions. For example, for student collaboration, students within an in-person classroom setting can simply face each other and work together at the same table on an assignment or task. For student collaboration to manifest online, multiple edtech tools are required. Edtech tools for online student collaboration could be in the form of a shared Google Doc, a backchannel like YoTeach! for chatting back and forth, or a breakout room in Zoom, Google Meet, or Microsoft Teams. With this said, the same edtech tools could be utilized in an in-person class session as the content they are working on is digitalized and can be collaboratively worked on in the same manner in-person as it can be worked on collaboratively by the online. Through this example, we are demonstrating that many of the same instructional strategies can be implemented in both online and in-person educational settings. As a result, regardless of whether schools can be open for in-person instruction, instruction can always be occurring continuously without any disruptions in a very similar manner for secondary schools over the course of the school year, which is how we can overcome many of the challenges presented by the toggled term.

The Toggled Term Instructional Model - An Instructional Model for Simultaneous and Continuous Learning			
Asynchronous Instruction Online (24/7) Learning Online Lectures/Content Screencast Videos, Hyperdocs/Slide Presentations, Interactive Asynchronous Slides, Student Collaboration, Independent Practice, Teacher Feedback & Communication, and Assessment			
Online Synchronous Instructional Strategies	**Synchronous Live Online Class Sessions**	**Synchronous In-Person Class Sessions on Campus**	**In-Person Instructional Strategies**
• Teacher Modeling/ Direct Instruction • Interactive Slideshows • Breakout Discussion Rooms • Student Backchannel Discussion • I Do, We Do, You Do • Student Collaboration • Independent Practice • Assessment			• Teacher Modeling/ Direct Instruction • Stations/ Centers (Independent Practice & Teacher Feedback) • Student Backchannel Discussion • Interactive Slideshows • I Do, We Do, You Do • Student Collaboration • Independent Practice • Assessment
HyFlex Live recorded class sessions or pre-recorded class sessions, or online activities that align with instruction that occurred during synchronous live class sessions			

Figure 12.1. The Toggled Term Instructional Model - An Instructional

Model for Simultaneous and Continuous Learning

Lastly, for this model to provide as much equity as possible for secondary students, there is an opportunity to alleviate some inequities like having to attend in-person or online during scheduled synchronous class sessions. For example, for students who cannot attend live synchronous sessions due to health concerns or personal circumstances, the HyFlex element of this model allows them to participate and engage in their classes beyond the asynchronous instruction provided. The HyFlex option allows teachers to design their courses in a manner that all students can participate in all aspects of the class. For example, teachers have the opportunity to record their synchronous live class sessions (whether they are online or in-person). Students can watch and engage with class sessions online or watch the recorded session later and participate in the same interactive slideshow or an alternative activity provided by their teacher. An example of what this looks like in practice is when a teacher provides a backchannel chatroom or an interactive bulletin board that prompts students regardless of whether they participated during the live class to share what they learned. Also, it allows students who completed the alternative activity to participate and interact with their classmates if the student did not attend the live in-person or online synchronous class session. In this light, teachers can design assignments and tasks students can complete that mirror to the best of their ability the activities that were presented during the live synchronous sessions. The alternative assignments and tasks can be geared towards meeting the same standards as the instruction provided in the synchronous live class sessions.

Conclusion

To have an instructional model that allows for continuous learning during the toggled term for secondary schools, we must utilize a model that incorporates the three components of asynchronous, synchronous, and HyFlex instruction to make this happen. As discussed in earlier chapters, teachers must know how to utilize a learning management system and several edtech tools to implement the Toggled Term

Instructional Model. This is key, as this capacity is required for secondary schools to be successful in moving forward as they navigate the toggled term. Ultimately, with this instructional model discussed in this chapter, it requires teachers to build an online instructional infrastructure, so instruction can take place online and in-person regardless of whether brick and mortar schools can be physically open throughout the school year.

Overall, the foundations to navigate the toggled term have been outlined in Part 1, 2, and 3 of this book. It is now time to focus on building the capacity to ensure we can navigate the toggled term and prepare to continue learning as the conditions our schools face will remain fluid for the foreseeable future. We now must utilize our professional learning network to ensure all secondary teachers have the ability to implement the instructional edtech, best practice strategies, and online and blended learning educational settings to ensure our students can learn continuously without disruption over the course of the school year.

CHAPTER 13

Professional Learning as an Educator Using Social Media - Your Social Knowledge Network is Your Net Worth

Educators must continue to learn to adapt to the current education landscape as online and blended learning instruction seem to be the most plausible form of instruction for the next 12 to 18 months. The good news is that more than ever before, educators have more resources for professional learning and the ability to network with experienced educators from around the world to share and consume information. The days from the past are gone when teachers have only their close colleagues in their grade level and content department at their school site and district administrators for professional development. More importantly, gone are the days of having a choice of not having to rely on professional learning networks to learn and grow as an educator. Today, it is not a choice not to continue to develop professionally as an educator, regardless of where you may be in your career. Educators must continue learning to put their students in the best positions to succeed in our ever-changing world. As George Couros, a famous innovator and trailblazer in education has noted, it is a personal choice to remain isolated as an educator because there are a plethora of resources online for professional development and opportunities to connect with best educators throughout our local community and the world (Couros, 2015).

Given the circumstance and the resources available to enhance your practices as an educator, teachers and administrators can create the best outcomes for their students by continuing to develop personally and by building their professional learning network. Through these efforts, we as an educational community can share our knowledge and experiences with others in the field to then implement within their districts, schools, and classrooms across the country and the world. Ultimately, this is what impact looks like when educators elect to improve their practice in the 21st-century.

To reiterate, teachers and administrators in today's educational landscape do not have a choice but to grow professionally and utilize social networks and the internet as resources to refine their craft. This is because education is changing and evolving faster than we have ever seen it before, especially during a pandemic like we are experiencing now throughout the world. As a result, teachers and administrators throughout the world have had to completely change their instructional models to facilitate learning in a matter of weeks and must continue to do so indefinitely. Consequently, there are significant disparities in knowhow for online learning, blended learning, and using technology by educators regardless of the level they teach. A monumental change like this can happen if all educators use the resources they have at their disposal and take the time to build capacity in their craft to successfully learn the practices required of them to navigate the toggled term.

Teachers and administrators should always want to utilize their school site and district for professional development. Still, they should also want to augment their professional learning and their professional learning network of teachers and administrators with social networks and internet resources that exponentially increase their ability to learn from educators throughout the world. To be a teacher or administrator who utilizes these extensive networks and resources to their fullest potential, we must have an "innovator's mindset" as described by George Couros to systematically take the information we learn and create new and better ideas. To break this down, we must have the mindset and "belief that the abilities, intelligence's, and talents are developed so that they can lead to the creation of new and better ideas" (Couros, 2015, p. 33).Thus, as we go through the topics throughout this chapter of building your own brand as an educator, using social media and the internet for professional learning and networking, and employing digital portfolios to develop an online presence to share and reflect our knowledge to others, keep the innovator's mindset in your thoughts.

By keeping the innovators' mindset in your thoughts, it can transform the way you take in information to use your own unique and creative ways to transform our classroom and world for our students and our profession as a whole. Also, by having an innovator's mindset, it can help teachers and administrators navigate the toggled term in the fall and beyond. In this same instance, the innovator's mindset can allow teachers and administrators to take on the challenge of transitioning back and forth between online and face to face instruction as an opportunity to innovate the very nature of education and to create creative solutions to the problems they encounter.

Building Your Own Brand as an Educator

Building a brand is vital as an educator because it represents who you are as a person and educator and what you can share with the world. As humans, we want to be known for who we are because we are looking for a purpose and intrinsically want to make an impact in some way or form. Think about it; we want to share who we are and what we can share with the world outside of the school and district we work at because learning is not constrained on where we work and live anymore. When thinking about developing professionally as a teacher or administrator, first think about how we can share your experience and expertise with others by taking a moment to ask yourself some questions about who you are as a person and educator.

- What values do you have?
- How can you invoke your value in what you do in person as well as online?
- What impactful insights and skills do you use with your students and school that you can also share with the global community of educators?

Creating our own personal brand allows us to show who we are as an educator and share our unique talents, experiences, and creativity to your colleagues within your school, district, and the global education community. By building a brand in education and sharing it with others, it will motivate us to continue to improve by reflecting on our craft. This will allow for a synthesis of our experiences and expertise as educators. As a result, this combination of experiences and expertise can be shared with the world. Simultaneously through this process, we build our capacity because we can take in what other educators have shared with the world, which can then be used to serve our students and school better. All of this is part of the process of building our own brand as educators.

Using Social Media to Build Your Social Network, Brand, and Professionally Develop

Social networks have transformed learning for teachers and administrators. Specifically, Twitter has allowed educators to connect with and learn from educators throughout the world. Prominent educators, as well as beginners, share their knowledge and experiences with others in the field. Generally, educators in the field share research articles, infographics, articles, and anecdotal experiences of scenarios with their students and colleagues as ways to share their knowledge, experiences, and innovations with others.

To organize topics on **Twitter**, **Linkedin**, and **Facebook**, #hastags are used to categorize topics and ideas shared with the public by social network users. The power of #hashtags has allowed for topics to be organized within categories, which can be accessed by anyone. Topics under a particular #hashtag can be searched by individual users who are curious about what is being discussed under a particular topic. Thus, to start, if a teacher or administrator wants to learn more about Special Education, they can search #SPED, #Specialeducation, #autism, #differentiatedinstruction, etc., as a means to see what others in the field are talking about and sharing resources out to the online community on topics related to Special Education.

Additionally, on Twitter, Twitter chats have evolved out of the use of #hashtags, which are time specified conversations or on-going conversations about a specific topic. Organizations, as well as networks of individuals, use Twitter chats as ways to share information regarding a specific to individuals within the social network in addition to others who wish to explore the conversation to learn more about the topic. For example, #edtechchat is a popular education technology Twitterchat, which explores new edtech being used in face to face and online classrooms. Browsing this #hashtag would allow us to see trending new topics on edtech as well as posts from prominent practitioners and experts in the field to glean knowledge from their helpful posts, links to content and resources, infographics, and videos. All of these facets are extremely helpful when looking to learn more about a particular topic to help refine your teaching practices.

To build your own brand on a social network to share your expertise and conduct professional development, make sure to follow prominent educators in the field you already know about their work. These prominent education figures can be individuals from our district, school, nation, and world. We can ultimately narrow the niche of education we want to focus on as an educator. For example, say you are a teacher who is passionate about edtech and Special Education. You can follow prominent researchers, teachers, and administrators in the field of educational technology and Special Education. Sometimes, they may even follow us back as a result. Also, when we follow a prominent person on Twitter in your specific niche area, look and see the educators who are following them and look to further expand your network by following their followers. Remember, individuals, even without a large following on Twitter, can provide very insightful content you can utilize in your classroom, school, and district. While looking at individuals to follow on Twitter, first look at their biographies on Twitter, Linkedin, and personal website/blogs, if available. Second, scroll through their Twitter feed to see if their content aligns with what you want to learn or your interests in the field. By doing this first initial research, it will help you determine who we would like to follow and learn from on Twitter. And you never know, individuals who we follow on Twitter may follow you back based on who you are and what you share to the world.

Lastly, to further build your own brand, share what you know to others. By posting engaging and useful content to your followers, you will gain more followers as well as follow more individuals as your professional learning network grows. Your posts could include daily experiences about your students and colleagues, what occurs at your classroom or school site that could be replicated elsewhere, blog posts, pertinent research, infographics, and thoughts about a specific topic. There are endless possibilities. At the end of the day, as long as the content you post is of interest to others, you can guarantee people within the education world will be reading what you are sharing over the Twitter feed. Thus, over time, you may become known on Twitter for producing content, engaging in Twitter chats, or talking about a topic with expertise like #edtech, #sped, #duallanguage, #sel, etc. that educators will find of interest and value to them.

Digital Portfolios

Beyond social media, to further share who we are and what we can bring to the table, developing a digital portfolio is a platform that can meet this end. Now, we have the ability to share the content and projects we have worked hard for over the course of our education and careers to be showcased to colleagues and the rest of the education community online. A digital portfolio intertwines the elements of a professional website, social media, blog, and YouTube Channel, to showcase who you are as an educator and person as well as demonstrate your professional learning over time. Online website platforms such as **Wordpress**, **Edublog**, **Weebly**, and **Google Sites** can consolidate all other edtech platforms (i.e., social media, professional website, YouTube page, etc.) onto one platform. What this does is allow educators throughout the world to find your small space on the internet dedicated to showing the world who you are and what you can share with them regarding your teaching strengths as well as areas you are learning and growing in.

Why do we want to share content and our accomplishments with the world? More than likely, we have built and created something that is valuable because we are all unique and provide talents the world can use. Thus, we can share valuable content with our colleagues, future employers, and the greater educational community, which will show them who we are and our expertise in the field.

Digital portfolios should include four critical areas. First, digital portfolios need to provide information about who you are. An "about page" should be one of the main pages on the digital portfolio that embeds your current resume' into the narrative page you are writing about yourself. This "about me" page includes your work experience, education, projects/publications, and hobbies. Second, if you have any specific projects or publications you want to share, create a page summarizing them or providing links to where they can be accessed. Third, digital portfolios can integrate our social media and be used as a home base where hyperlinks can be provided directly to their public feed for the public to view. Fourth, digital portfolios can be used as a platform to create content and share content throughout our social network. Some of the most popular ways to create content are through writing blog posts, producing videos on YouTube, and sharing recent publications.

If you do not already have a digital portfolio, look to see what digital portfolios are out there before building it. Emulating the structure of digital portfolios of others is a great way to start. Over time, your digital portfolio will diverge and become unique as you build more content that relates to who you are and your specific talents as an educator. Take a look at some prominent digital portfolios of educators and professionals from all various fields of work in education and beyond:

- **www.georgecouros.ca**
- **www.cultofpedagogy.com**
- **www.daveburgess.com**
- **www.matthewrhoads.com**
- **www.carnaghiteachingportfolio.weebly.com**
- **www.charlesdaoud.com**

Conclusion

George Couros, in an *Innovator's Mindset,* provides a detailed explanation and graphic illustrating what the networked teacher should be doing to continue improving their craft and building their own brand as an educator. According to Couros (2015), be the networked teacher, it includes the components of microblogging, having relationships with colleagues and the local community, utilizing popular media and the internet for professional development, social networking and developing relationships with educators throughout the world, and technology instructional integration (p. 197). Besides just teachers, the components of a networked teacher can include administrators and all other roles educators hold, regardless of whether they are in K-12 or at the university-level. Thus, every educator, regardless of position and level, needs always to continue learning, networking, and sharing their experiences and content with others in the global education community.

At the end of the day, it is up to us as educators to continue to learn, network, and share our brand with the local and online educational community regardless of our position in the world of education. In today's world, there is so much information available that it is merely not a choice not to seek it out. Gone are many of the barriers to accessing critical information and experiences to help us grow as educators. Moving forward, think about having an innovator's mindset like discussed at the beginning of this chapter to be ready for the realities of what a toggled term will bring in the fall and beyond. With this mindset, confronting these challenges will be more inviting.

Additionally, with this mindset, educators will be in the position to take in the new information systematically we learn and create new and better ideas for our district, school, and students to weather this crisis and thrive long-term. Ultimately, all educators can add so much to our students' experiences regardless of the education setting we are in the future because all educators have unique talents, experiences, and the innate creativity to innovate and problem solve. Thus, from this moment on, have an innovator's mindset and continue to learn and build relationships through your professional learning network. It will be one of the single most important factors in moving forward and being the best educator possible for our students now and in the future.

Part 3. Conclusion

Ultimately, as Part 3 of this book closes, let us take a look back at what we learned. The purpose of Part 3 was to begin the conversation on how we can initially reopen schools. Then, the discussion shifted to learning about blended learning, which can be utilized as the instructional foundation for navigating the toggled term. In Chapter 12, we built onto the blended learning instructional model by introducing the Toggled Term Instructional Model, which allows for continuous learning throughout the school year as it is an instructional model that can toggle back and forth between fully online learning and blended learning educational settings. Lastly, Part 3 ended by putting us in the mindset to begin focusing on professional development as we prepare to navigate the challenges presented by the toggled term.

As the evolution of the conversation begins for opening schools, there are many variables to assess in developing plans to reopen. Social distancing and heightened hygiene protocols, staggered scheduling, and blended learning instructional models seem inevitable to be beginning sometime in the fall semester and beyond for the next 12 to 18 months until a vaccine is readily available. Schools must also evaluate how to meet the needs of their most vulnerable students who require the highest level of education services. Additionally, professional development is key to bolstering innovation during this time. Providing educators an incentive to share what they know as well as create the necessary professional learning networks to glean as much information as they can from the education community is critical in being able to take on challenges that could last 12 to 18 months.

Opportunities already exist to learn. Right now, opportunities already exist where the majority of U.S. districts and schools can observe school systems around the world. Even within the U.S. (i.e., Montana opened their schools first in early May 2020), we can observe and evaluate schools that have already begun to reopen in some capacity for face to face instruction. Since these opportunities exist, it is essential educators in our country observe, evaluate, ask questions, and learn from the very schools that reopened. Also, we can learn from the educators themselves in our backyard and across the world on how to create innovative solutions to the complex problems schools face as they reopen amid a pandemic. Ultimately, much of what districts and schools observed and evaluated from others who have begun reopening during the late spring and the summer of 2020 will be utilized to drive the decision-making processes for how schools can plan to navigate the toggled term.

Now, the conversation shifts to how districts and schools can navigate the toggled term and beyond as we move into the future. Many questions exist as more thought and planning is put into preparing for the 2020-2021 school year. What will be the realities in the fall and beyond? What types of problems will exist? How will teachers and administrators adapt to these changes? Will staggered scheduling ensure students, teachers, and staff are safe? Will blended learning be an equitable form of instruction for secondary education? Will districts and schools be able to transition between blended learning and fully online instruction multiple times within a semester if the realities of the toggled term come to fruition? These are all critical questions that must be consistently addressed and assessed. Thus, the following conclusion in Part 4 will focus on navigating these questions, the realities of a toggled term, and the very future of K-12 education in the U.S.

PART 4

Conclusion - Navigating the Future of K-12 Within a Toggled Term

The realities of the fall semester and beyond seem unimaginable a year ago. Who knew that the second half of the spring semester would be taught online? Our 150 years of traditional brick and mortar education has been rocked to its very core. Over the next 12 to 18 months, K-12 education will be completely revamped to adapt to the conditions this pandemic has brought, and there may be everlasting effects. Education has given our country and the rest of the world hope for the future. It will be our bridge towards a recovery. Not only will it allow for economic recovery, but it will also uplift our communities and bring people together once again.

There is one big question overhanging all plans to reopen schools: how will secondary educators navigate the future for the long-term? It is time to address this question further as well as bring forth some ideas of how to manage the toggled term and evaluate the challenges it will bring to secondary education. Furthermore, in this conclusion, the realities of the toggled term will be outlined in length. The discussion will then shift towards how future longitudinal plans should be developed and how all stakeholders can be involved in the process. Then, our conversation will move towards how teachers and administrators in secondary schools can manage the toggled term. Finally, a framework on how to navigate the toggled will be outlined, which districts and schools can employ to help them navigate the toggled term throughout the 2020-2021 school year and beyond. Within this framework, a district and school's current mission/vision and organizational structures can be integrated together to put teachers and students in the best position to be successful in moving between blended learning models of instruction and fully online instruction over a long-term basis. To round out Part 4 and the conclusion of this book, there will be an honest conversation about the future of K-12 education, which provides several implications for secondary schools and their educators. Overall, the future remains fluid and ever-changing. Even with overarching uncertainty, we have educators who will be able to innovate and create positive outcomes for students across the country as we move into the fall and beyond.

The Realities of a Toggled Term

As a recurring theme throughout this book, the toggled term is inevitable and will hit various parts of the country more so than others. There will be times when entire districts and schools will shut down their blended face-to-face instruction and move to online instruction entirely for days, weeks, or even months. It is inevitable a student or teacher gets infected with COVID-19 once districts and schools initially reopen for some form of face to face instruction. It has already happened in schools around the world that have initially reopened. What will happen when that occurs? Will the school or the entire district have to close and move online when this happens? Will there be protocols in place to monitor student health upon entering schools and mechanisms for contact tracing? God forbid, a student or teacher dies of this disease after the schools reopening. What will happen as a result? In a morbid sense, districts and schools will have to plan for and endure these types of scenarios.

States and districts will have different plans in place for when a student, teacher, or staff get infected. When this inevitably does happen, schools would be wise to close down for days or even weeks to disinfect, clean, and contact trace to ensure the spread stops within its jurisdiction. Thus, as a result of this, the toggle will be triggered. When this toggled is triggered by a positive case(s), online instruction should begin immediately, which means learning can be continuous regardless of the local health conditions.

Toggling Between Closing and Reopening Schools. How many times could a toggle take place during a semester? It will depend. As alluded to at the beginning of this conversation, a toggle between educational settings will be triggered more often in some districts and schools than in others. Districts and schools in population-dense cities have a higher probability of infections. However, a triggered toggle to move online due to positive cases being found at a school site could happen anywhere and at any time. Short and long-term preparations will need to be in place for quickly closing and then reopening after disinfection and contact tracing have occurred. Ultimately, testing capacities will need to be ramped up to test anyone suspected of being in contact with the positive case(s).

Additionally, for students and teachers who have been in contact with an individual at the school site who has tested positive, how will classes and learning take place for those individuals who have to be quarantined for two weeks as a result of contacting tracing? Questions also exist regarding how long the initial closing, cleaning, and contact tracing will take and how much will it cost each time to close and reopen a school and district's brick and mortar facilities each time a toggle is triggered? We also must consider the entire organization and community as a whole. How will administrators, teachers, staff, students, and parents handle each toggle? Over time, there could be pushback.

The more prepared and coherent the toggle strategies within the district and school plans will determine if school organizational systems can be maintained and maneuvered through the process of continuously going back and forth between virtual online and face to face educational settings. Communication regarding online and face to face settings, instructional models, and school-based resources (i.e., school nutrition, social work, mental health) will need to be extensive and revisited over the long-term and given to the local educational community before the semester begins. Furthermore, when the school reopens in any capacity, communication must be constant and transparent on school safety in any event a COVID-19 infection occurs (i.e., information on school disinfection and contact tracing). By being prepared, schools can communicate and then execute a toggle to close down face to face for online instruction. If successful during the first toggle to close down temporarily and move virtually for some time, it will heighten the morale of all school community stakeholders as well as create more trust in the school community. Additionally, it will provide a successful blueprint going forward when subsequent closures and reopening toggles occur in the future.

Consequently, a toggle will also reoccur when schools shift back from online instruction to a blended learning setting when it is deemed safe to begin easing back into face to face instruction after a closure. In the same way as toggling to virtual online settings, there will have to be many organizational systems in place that will revert back from an almost fully online infrastructure within days or weeks. These services and resources a school provides will have to ease back into face to face contact and instruction for each reopening. Beyond having the organizational systems in place to initially reopen, there must be trust from students, parents, and the local community that the school and district will be safe to reopen after a subsequent closure. Also, having the resources to toggle to reopen the physical facilities will be needed. With each subsequent toggle from closure to reopen, there will be a higher cost to reopen because the physical facilities of a school campus must reopen in contrast to maintaining a virtual online campus. Supplies, disinfecting/cleaning, and paying once again for full utilities will have to be outlined within the plan to reopen the facilities during a toggle.

Beyond supplies and reopening the physical campus, there must be a review of all COVID-19 protocols. A thorough review of social distancing and hygiene protocols will likely have to be reviewed once again before a school campus will be allowed to reopen. Most importantly, all health guidelines from the federal, state, and local county/city must be met. Therefore, communication and collaboration with these authorities are critical before any initial reopening, and subsequent reopening can occur after toggles are triggered.

How a Toggled Term May Affect Students and Teachers. The realities of a toggled semester on student learning will be immense. Students will be strained emotionally, academically, and socially due to new policies like staggered scheduling, social distancing, temperature checks, the wearing of masks, possible contact tracing efforts, hyper hygienic practices, and the very nature of changing educational settings. Besides, the realities of students living in tough family situations amid difficult economic times, sporadic childcare, and inconsistencies with the school routine will be topics that policymakers will also have to address when developing long-term plans to navigate a toggled term. As a result, students will be affected in all aspects of their lives, especially with how they learn. Younger students will likely face more academic regression when a toggle is triggered when a blended learning environment transforms into a solely online educational setting. Older students will be affected similarly. But they will be burdened with more responsibilities like childcare and the possibility of having to work to support their families during the midst of a deep economic recession. Remember, this is just the tip of the iceberg.

For teachers, they will be affected by many of the same reality's students will face when schools begin initially reopening for some form of face to face instruction. Over the course of several months, the very nature of the job of being an educator has completed changed. Instructionally, the spring semester shifted instruction to being solely online. Now, teachers and administrators alike will need to learn how to effectively teach in a blended learning model as well as be ready at a moment's notice to shut down and move entirely to online instruction. More so than ever, besides being educators teaching students skills and content, teachers will take on additional responsibilities to ensure all the new protocols like social distancing, temperature checks, mask-wearing, and hygienic practices are being enforced and followed in schools.

Finally, on top of the new responsibilities, teachers and administrators will have a fear of reentering a campus due to the safety concerns relating to COVID-19. Older teachers and administrators, especially those who may have an underlying health problem, will be fearful of their health. Through all of this, there will be times where teachers will have to completely transition their blended learning classrooms to become entirely online for a period when a closure toggle is triggered. Then, subsequently, a similar transition will occur once again when schools toggle to reopen for some form of blended face to face instruction.

Developing Future Longitudinal Plans - A Framework Forward

The realities going forward for all will be tough to overcome. If districts and schools are pragmatic and develop plans that are nearsighted and farsighted for how to initially reopen for face to face instruction as well as the possibility of toggling during a semester, there will be a level of success for districts, schools, teachers, and students. When schools initially reopen for face to face instruction, there will be much less of a possibility of having to close the physical campus for long periods of time (i.e., week(s) rather than months) when a toggle is triggered. If plans are developed and successfully executed, the lives of students, teachers, administrators, and staff will be safer, more learning will occur, morale will not plummet, and there will be higher levels of trust from stakeholders within the school community. Thus, when thinking about developing and refining longitudinal plans to counter the realities that relate to a toggled term, all stakeholders within a school community need to be involved in designing and refining plans to initially reopen as well as how to toggle throughout the school year effectively.

Ultimately, each local district and school will have different needs. This means districts and schools cannot fully imitate others because they have local variables to work through. Yet, foundationally, having a workable framework in place to develop plans will help districts and schools initially reopen and have the capacity to toggle. As a result, a school reform framework is needed for districts and schools to utilize as a foundational piece to allow them to navigate the challenges presented by this crisis.

One successful framework that stands out for school reform is Michael Fullan and Joanne Quinn's (2016) Coherence Framework. Fullan and Quinn's framework has transformed districts and schools throughout North America because it allows for the flexibility of local conditions to be integrated into the framework's structural components. Fundamentally, Fullan and Quinn (2016) argue the components of a focused direction, with internal and external accountability, cultivating collaborative cultures, and deepening learning must be in place to be the drivers of change to "have a shared depth of understanding about the purpose and nature" of school reform (p. 14). Thus, this reality is apparent. To navigate the toggled term, an element of school reform is needed for developing and refining plans to initially reopen and toggle between various educational settings because the nature of how K-12 education will operate will be fundamentally different moving forward into the future.

Now, it is time to see how secondary schools can utilize this framework for navigating the toggled term. For the first step in formulating this framework, districts and schools must plan to have a purpose in why they are implementing new protocols like social distancing, staggered scheduling, blended learning, and the like for when schools initially reopen. Communicating the purpose to all stakeholders and the local community will be one of the single most important strategies to ensure everyone is informed of what is going on and have the rationale behind the short and long-term plans being formulated. The overarching purpose of "why" needs to be accompanied by a clear strategy outlining goals, mechanisms for measuring the outlined goals, and protocols for how a district and school can initially reopen as well as toggle back and forth throughout a school year. During this time, school and district leaders need to support collaborative cultures and participate as learners in the process by building "vertical and horizontal capacity and integration" (Fullan & Quinn, 2016, p. 39). What this looks like is that entire school sites and districts should have similar procedures in place for safety and instruction, as well as professional development, to ensure it is implemented for organizational transparency and coherence. Ultimately, through this process, it illustrates that this is managing a shift to a new pathway of change from the current state to the future state to allow for the school system to navigate new scenarios and variables presented by the current conditions present.

Collaborative and cultivating cultures are going to be needed, as the situation remains fluid. Toggling will require collaboration and innovation. There is no way around it. Thus, the second step of this framework that can be adopted involves building capacity through on-going professional development and professional learning networks, collaborative work as grade levels, departments, and entire schools, and accepting that this will be a time of learning and growth (Fullan & Quinn, 2016). This collaboration and capacity building looks like creating learning partners across the district and its school(s), sustained focus on the goals of the school and district during the toggled term, and cycles of structured inquiry and reflection by administrators, teachers, students, and the local community. What this looks like in our context of a toggled term is the mobilization of teachers, departments, administrators, and school systems to develop models of instruction, like blended learning, together with the steps towards its implementation. This involves online training and coaching to facilitate any form of implementation. Following implementation, inquiry and reflection will follow implementation to determine what steps can be conducted to improve as the school year goes on. Additionally, within this framework, it also provides teachers and administrators with the opportunity to have flexibility and freedom of how it can be implemented for the educational setting (Fullan & Quinn, 2016).

The third step of the framework is securing internal and external accountability from teachers, staff, administrators, and the surrounding community is predicated on the moral imperative. To synthesize Fullan and Quinn's (2016) moral imperative into our current scenario of planning to reopen schools initially as well as for the possibility of a toggled term, it relates to establishing an overarching purpose for reopening schools and maintaining continuous learning. Within this purpose, the personal values of teachers and staff are interwoven with the characteristics of persistence and resilience. To foster the moral imperative, while developing and refining plans to reopen and to manage the toggled term, relationship building with all stakeholders is critical (Fullan & Quinn, 2016). Even this will include people who disagree, who are skeptical, and who are even cynical of reopening schools in any capacity or individuals who want a full-on traditional setting. These individuals must be listened to and given opportunities to be part of the process. Beyond relationship building and cultivating engagement from all stakeholders, school and district leaders need to be transparent and collaborative while developing, implementing, and refining their initial reopening and toggle plans. In this same manner, their strategies need to be clear and pragmatic, and organizational inefficiencies need to be reduced so that each toggle can occur as seamlessly as possible (Fullan & Quinn, 2016).

The last aspect of this framework to integrate into developing plans to navigate the toggled term is deep learning. With blended learning in play as one of the most viable instructional models to be utilized during a toggled term, it can be the overarching form of instruction that can then teach the competencies of deep learning. Deep learning fundamentally is taking knowledge from experience and incorporates it across a range of skills and attributes, which include communication, critical thinking, collaboration, creativity, character, and citizenship (Fullan & Quinn, 2016, p. 89-90). Ultimately, online, blended learning, and HyFlex instructional models, as outlined in the Toggled Term Instructional Model, can provide opportunities in secondary schools to teach the six competencies of deep learning (i.e., 6C's) in online and face to face settings. Due to these educational settings, the Toggled Term Instructional Model can incorporate, to align directly to 21st-century learning, as the six competencies allow students to create their own understanding of the continually evolving and fluid world we live in today. To incorporate these competencies in an instructional, Fullan and Quinn (2016) suggest developing a common instructional language and pedagogical practices. By doing this, it ensures transparency and alignment exists from one school to another as well as each level of organization within a school (i.e., grade levels, departments, etc.). Furthermore, in the context of a toggled term, this common instructional language and pedagogical practices could include how edtech tools are used and intertwined with instructional strategies for face to face and online instruction. Also, within the instructional and pedagogy practices instituted, protocols such as social distancing, school site/classroom hygiene, staggered scheduling, and procedures to organizationally shift one way or another when a toggle is trigged should be included.

To ensure these new elements of an instructional language, pedagogical practices, and COVID-19 protocols are implemented, Fullan and Quinn (2016) recommend horizontal and vertical professional development across the entire school system to create organizational transparency and capacity before any implementation of these practices occurs. In this same instance, during a time of continuous change, Fullan and Quinn (2016) suggest fostering instructional risk-taking as a means to innovate and improve to create the best outcomes for students as possible. Districts and schools need to allow teachers and administrators to explore and find solutions to many of the instructional challenges that are presented by the realities of a toggled term. Furthermore, if instructional risk-taking is embedded in the culture of the school, there will be an openness to collaborate and work together to be creative and share instructional creativity with others.

Navigating the Toggled Term Utilizing Fullan and Quinn's Coherence Framework		
Focused Direction • Clear strategy and plan that is consistently communicated to all stakeholders. • Measurable goals to address reopening and closing toggles. • Implementing blending and online learning instructional models simultaneously by employing the Toggled Term Instructional Model. • Health policies and student safety are interwoven into all goals and strategies.		**Accountability** • Buy-in from stakeholders and the community on the schools reopen/closure toggle strategies • In-person/onlinecheck-ins from leaders. • Evidence of professional growth. • Relationship development with students, parents, teachers, administrators, and staff. • Ensure all teachers have an understanding of how to toggle their classrooms between educational settings.
	Navigating the Toggled Term	
Moral Imperative • Staff trust and belief in district/school toggle goals. • Personal values and beliefs of teachers and staff are integrated into district/school goals. • Community trust in the goals of the school/district. • Develop relationships with the school community	**Collaborative Cultures** • Flexibility and freedom to innovate. • Developing learning partnerships with colleagues in-person and online through professional learning networks. • Focus on the goals of the school/district. • Reflection on learning.	**Deep Learning** • Focus on the 6's for 21st-century learners. • Develop a common instructional language for blended learning and online learning. • Focused pedagogical practices. • Vertical and horizontal professional development. • Foster instructional risk-taking by teachers.

Figure Part 4.1. Incorporating the Coherence Framework During the Toggled Term

Fullan and Quinn's Coherence Framework, as illustrated in Figure Part 4.1 above, is a start to thinking about how districts and schools can adjust their organizational systems to withstand the realities presented by the toggled term. Frameworks like Fullan and Quinn's should be considered to combat these challenges because they are flexible to the local challenges and variables districts and schools may face. Other frameworks may exist that can provide districts and schools with flexibility. However, any other framework should contain the elements Fullan and Quinn's framework provides because navigating the toggled term will require a purposeful and focused direction, accountability of teachers and staff held together by the moral imperative, collaborative culture to problem solve and innovate, and deep learning propelled by a blended learning and online instructional model that is aligned with the six competencies of 21st-century learning.

Managing the Toggled Term

Managing the toggled term will have its challenges. Yet, they are surmountable if future short and long-term plans take into consideration several vital challenges relating to the toggled term. This will be especially true when the first toggle occurs after the initial reopening to close down and move virtually online for a given time. As a result, all future plans will need to be developed to consider moving entire districts and school's organizational systems and instructional models online to a virtual setting. Luckily, this had occurred once before because the vast majority of districts and schools closed to move to online-only distance learning instruction during the spring of 2020. The difference this time around will be the amount of time the physical school facilities will be closed when a toggle to close the campus is triggered.

Logistically, depending on the school's physical size, it could take several days to a few weeks to thoroughly disinfect the campus. Also, time must be taken into consideration for being able to trace contacts of students, teachers, or staff who have been infected in addition to widespread testing that must be taken place to ensure the campus is safe to reopen. Thus, a possible toggle between a blended learning educational setting incorporating elements of face to face instruction and fully online instruction could last several days, to weeks, or even as long as a month depending on the local health conditions.

Educators will also have to problem solve for the many families who may not want their students to return to school initially to participate in in-person blended learning. Therefore, all instructional models need to include students who will work solely online from home and students who are quarantined over a given time as a result of having contact with a positive case. As a result, during the preparation for the fall and beyond, future plans need to take into consideration the turnaround time a toggle may take. The best possible route is to develop and implement plans that have brick and mortar and online organizational systems in place simultaneously to make each transition seamless.To continue to expand and facilitate this conversation, the financial, trust, teacher/staff morale, instructional, and safety implications a toggled term presents will be outlined. These are all significant facets that will need to be in place for any district and school to navigate the toggled term successfully.

Financial. Budget preparations should include projections of how much it will cost to shut down a physical school site and how much it will cost to reopen. Embedded within budgets should be funds allocated to projections of how many times a district and school may toggle throughout the semester and school year. By having these auxiliary funds in place, it will ensure erratic spending does not take place when a toggle occurs. Thus, spending projections will ensure the necessary supplies, especially the cleaning and hygiene supplies (i.e., masks, face shields, disinfecting soaps, temperature thermometers, etc.) will be already funded and in storage before the school year begins.

Trust. Trust from the staff, parents, students, and the local community will be vital for reopening after the first toggled closure occurs. Districts and schools must prepare mechanisms of how to immediately communicate with teachers, students, staff, and the greater community if a toggle needs to occur. Transparency will be a necessity for all stakeholders in a school community from the beginning of the school year and onwards to take on "what if" scenarios relating to how a toggle occurs and what situations will prompt a toggle to occur. Ultimately, trust will be built if districts and schools are upfront about these processes and can communicate immediately with stakeholders once a toggle is triggered.

Teacher and Staff Morale. Another aspect that needs to be addressed will be teacher and staff morale. With every toggle that occurs, morale will take a hit. Therefore, in the initial plans to make schools safe for face to face instruction, teachers and staff will need to be included in the decision-making process in addition to community members to have buy-in from the majority of the schools. Morale, in this context, links directly to the moral imperative outlined when discussing Fullan and Quinn's (2016) Coherence Framework. To establish the buy-in to propel morale, relationship building, and interweaving the values of the teachers and staff into the vision for the school's plan to reopen initially, will go a long way. This trust or lack thereof will be evident when a toggle to close and move online is triggered after the school's initial reopening to some capacity of blended learning.

Instruction. Managing instruction will be another hurdle to overcome. Even in a blended learning educational setting, there will still be elements of online instruction. First, initial reopening and long-term plans need to outline the expectations for what this blended learning model will look like once the school initially reopens. Then, to ensure these expectations are shown, professional development needs to be aligned directly to the expectations. Elements of edtech will also need to be addressed. Will the same platforms used in the spring be used in the fall? Will there be any training regarding what form of instruction will accompany the mainstream edtech tools selected by the district?

Additionally, how will assessing student progress and providing feedback look like throughout the year regardless of the educational setting? Which instructional practices will need to be etched in stone and not be changed if a toggle is triggered? On top of grading practices, the student and family accountability piece will also be an area that must be addressed. What will be the consequences of attending face to face days as well as not participating in online learning if a school toggles fully online for an extended time? Will the grades of students suffer as a result? Thus, each of these questions will need to be addressed in plans to reopen schools to prepare teachers for the instructional realities a toggled term presents.

Safety. Student, teacher, and staff safety and mental health will also be at the forefront of being able to manage the toggled term. Safety protocols like social distancing, staggered schedules, hygienic practices, masks, daily disinfecting, desk shields, temperature checks, and personnel movement plans within the school facility will all have to be employed. On top of these initial safety protocols, there must be consistent communication and collaboration with local health authorities to ensure an infrastructure exists for these protocols to be implemented. A supply chain of masks, disinfectants, thermometers, desk and face shields, COVID-19 testing kits, and medical personnel will be needed and readily available to support districts before any reopening is possible. Ongoing implementation and enforcement of policies and the availability to test and contact tracing will be paramount for the safety of students, teachers, staff, and administrators. Any lapses could result in infections and subsequent closures. Therefore, physical safety needs to take a front seat in managing the toggled term. Simply put, lives are at stake.

For the mental health component, a collaboration between districts and schools with local mental health providers will need to be exponentially increased. Upon arrival at a reopened school, students of all ages may require mental health services due to beingaway from school for months. At the current capacity before the crisis, there is not the capacity to meet the mental health needs of students, teachers, and staff. Thus, remote counseling will need to be increased along with other mental health supports provided within the mainstream curriculum. Training teachers, administrators, and support staff in socioemotional learning exercises could be part of the equation in addressing some of these challenges presented by student mental health.

Overall, managing the realities of the toggled term are immense. Included in the plans to initially reopen schools and longitudinal plans to navigate the toggled term should be many of the elements that have been discussed. Yet, there are many unforeseen challenges ahead that will require innovation, collaboration, and the ability to transform the organizational systems of districts and schools. While the future cannot be predicted, being as prepared as possible is required to take on the challenges ahead to ensure some level of success. Success first and foremost will always be student, teacher, and staff safety. Then, if a form of quality instruction can be sustained for as many students as possible throughout the next 12 to 18 months until the threat of COVID-19 is lowered or diminished, it can be considered a success.

The Future of K-12 Education

The future of K-12 education is unpredictable and fluid. There is no question funding for K-12 education will be at the forefront of how the future for the institution will pan out over the next 12 to 18 months. Immense amounts of funding will be required to reopen districts and schools. More so than ever before, will funding be needed to make schools the foundation for our nation's economic recovery? At this point, dramatic budget cuts have begun at the state level due to shortages in tax revenues. More federal funding is possible but cannot be guaranteed. Ultimately, funding will be fundamental in any success to initially reopening schools, maintaining safety protocols, ensuring quality instruction continues, and successfully navigating the toggled term.

Beyond funding, instruction will utilize some form of blended learning over the course of the next 12 to 18 months. Edtech will be embedded within this model of instruction as a learning management system will be the center of all content created by teachers regardless of grade level. Many edtech tools will be implemented for online and face to face instruction. Educators will become much more creative with synthesizing the technology with instructional best practices. As the trend of technological integration continues to accelerate, we may see much more technology integration within classrooms once face to face instruction returns full time once the crisis is over. In secondary schools, this will be the most apparent as edtech will be the foundation of all instruction going forward. Additionally, many districts and schools may begin using a blended learning model full time to personalize learning as well as consolidate costs over time if it is a successful instructional model during next fall and beyond.

Teachers and administrators will be much more technology-savvy, and a new generation of instructional innovation could take place during this time and over the next few years. Currently, there are a plethora of edtech tools that can be harnessed to personalize and differentiate instruction as well as collect data on student progress. Education was already in the midst of a transition towards a more personalized learning approach before the crisis began. Data collection and analysis will continue to help target decisions driving instruction while differentiated instruction will be evermore present as instruction becomes more personalized. Consequently, teachers and administrators can utilize multiple measures of academic progress through continuous data collection on individual students, entire classes, grade levels, across schools, and throughout districts.

Equity and access and education inequality will likely increase over the next few days as a result of this crisis. Budget cuts, technology access and training, and built up student learning regressions from school closures will make this much more evident than before the crisis. Poorer districts and schools will experience this the most in contrast to wealthy districts and schools that will be able to weather the crisis. Federal and state governments will have to address these issues as disparities will continue to grow unless government intervention takes place. Massive funding programs and the reevaluation of how local school districts are funded may need to be revisited. Thus, equity and access should be center stage as schools reopen. Teachers and educational interest groups will need to continue their fight from the past two years to ensure funding is not cut so disparities will not increase across schools in our country.

After the crisis unfolds, there may be a push to consolidate public K-12 districts and schools across the U.S. Charter schools may grow in the short term as they may advertise they are best equipped to provide students with blended learning and online instruction. Also, they may be able to toggle back and forth between a blended learning model and online instruction more effectively than districts because of their size and the vastly fewer regulations they must abide by to operate. Also, if blended learning turns out to be successful for the vast majority of schools during the crisis, there is a real possibility districts may consolidate their brick and mortar facilities and the number of teachers employed. Secondary schools may see the brunt of this because there will be significant growth in alternative education pathways. This will be because the blended learning and online learning models require less physical space and, ultimately, fewer teachers to implement. Additionally, steep budget cuts may be a consistent variable in play that will push districts to make cuts and consolidate as state revenues will be depleted until the economy begins to recover.

The function of K-12 education may continue to evolve into a more personalized educational approach as a result of the innovation seen during this crisis. With the edtech integration into instruction as well as the continuous availability of online content, teachers may be able to focus on personalizing instruction to students more so than ever before. Blended learning will significantly impact this evolution towards personalized learning. Face to face class sessions may evolve to help to focus on students who are in the most need. At the same time, online instruction may accelerate the ability of students to move through K-12 education at their own pace versus being constrained to yearly grade advances. To illustrate, primary school may include the most face to face instruction. Then, as students get older, face to face instruction may not be as needed every single school day. In middle school and high school, students may only need to attend two to three days a week, while the rest of their instruction could be based online. Students at these higher-grade levels may have varying amounts of face to face time based on their academic needs. Therefore, as we can see, the very nature of how K-12 education functions may push towards more personalized education.

Conclusion

In the end, K-12 education will be the pillar that will help our nation and nations around the world recover economically from the COVID-19 crisis—investing in our student's future yields the most dividends overtime for our economy and the health of our democracy. Thus, massive investment is needed to allow schools to reopen safely initially and to be able to toggle back and forth between face to face and online instruction effectively. If investment and pragmatic preparation do not occur over the summer of 2020, the fall and beyond could be catastrophic, resulting in further academic regression of our future generations and the disintegration of the K-12 education system. However, if this is done with strategic planning and investment, schools will be a sanctuary and an economic engine that will transform our country.

By evaluating the contents of this book, we hope that secondary teachers, administrators, and the broader school community have a further generalized understanding of the components needed to see how schools function in this climate as well as how to develop plans to reopen and navigate the toggled term. Many challenges lie ahead. Yet, the challenges can certainly be overcome by educators across this country. Educators are capable of massive change and will innovate to find creative solutions to the problems K-12 education faces amid this crisis. Most importantly, educators will be the pillars of hope for their students and their local school community to rebuild and move towards a new tomorrow.

References

Alexander, B. (2020). *Early signs of fall 2020: Three paths, three scenarios for higher education.* Retrieved 5 May 2020, from https://bryanalexander.org/

Afflerbach, P., Hurt, M., & Cho, B. Y. (2020). Reading comprehension strategy instruction. *Handbook of Strategies and Strategic Processing*, 99.

Archer, A., & Hughes, C. (2011). *Explicit instruction: Effective and efficient teaching.* NY: Guilford Publications.

Beatty, B.M. (2019). *Costs and benefits for hybrid-flexible courses and programs: Is the value worth the effort associated with Hybrid-Flexible course implementation?* In B.J. Beatty (Ed.), Hybrid-Flexible Course Design. Edtech Books. Retrieved from https://edtechbooks.org/hyflex/power_SDL

O'Brien, J., Lawrence, N., & Green, K. (2014). To war or not? Engaging middle school students in an ongoing online discussion. *The Social Studies,* 105(2), 101–107.

Borup, J., Stevens, M. A., & Hasler Waters, L. (2015). Parent and student perceptions of parent engagement at a cyber charter high school. *Online Learning*, 19(5). https://doi.org/10.1017/CBO9781107415324.004

Butcher, N., & Wilson-Strydom, M. (2008). *Technology and open learning: The potential of open education resources for K-12 education.* (pp. 725-745). Boston, MA: Springer US. doi:10.1007/978-0-387-73315-9_42

Burkins, J. M., & Yaris, K. (2016). *Who's doing the work?: How to say less so readers can do more.* Stenhouse Publishers: Portland, ME.

Centers for Disease Control. (2020). *Implementation of mitigation strategies for communities with local COVID-19 transmission.* Cdc.gov. Retrieved 13 May 2020, from https://www.cdc.gov/coronavirus/2019-ncov/downloads/community-mitigation-strategy.pdf

CommonLit. *(2020). About. Retrieved 15 June 2020, from https://www.commonlit.org/about?gclid=Cj0KCQjwuJz3BRDT ARIsAMg-HxULulA-mkqSq_U96_GcQ9qhkIeIzJGv16-p15QQUvtLcw8a8r8HB60aAlZYEALw_wcB*

Couros, G. (2015). *The innovator's mindset: Empower learning, unleash talent, and lead a culture of creativity.* San Diego, CA: Dave Burgess Consulting, Inc.

Centers for Disease Control and Prevention. (2020). *Communities, Schools, Workplaces, & EventsCenters for Disease Control and Prevention.* Retrieved 20 May 2020, from https://www.cdc.gov/coronavirus/2019-ncov/community/schools-childcare/schools.html

COVID-19 Guidance and Resources - Child Development (CA Dept of Education). (2020). Cde.ca.gov. Retrieved 13 May 2020, from https://www.cde.ca.gov/sp/cd/re/elcdcovid19.asp

Drexler, W. (2010). *The networked student: A design-based research case study of student constructed personal learning environments in a middle school science course* (Doctoral dissertation, University of Florida).

Drexler, W. (2010). The networked student model for construction of personal learning environments: Balancing teacher control and student autonomy. *Australasian Journal of Educational Technology*, 26(3), 369-385.

EdCal. (2020). *Taskforce presses for solutions to the digital divide.* Retrieved 17 May 2020, from https://edcal.acsa.org/task-force-presses-for-solutions-to-digital-divide

Edpuzzle. *(2020). About us. Retrieved 15 June 2020, from https:// edpuzzle.com/about*

Ferdig, R., Kennedy, K. *(2018). Handbook of research on K-12 online and blended learning (Second Edition) (Version 1).* Carnegie Mellon University. https://doi.org/10.1184/R1/6686813.v1

Flipgrid. *(2020). Empower every voice. Retrieved 15 June 2020, from https://info.flipgrid.com/*

Fullan, M., Senge, P. M. (2010). *All systems go: The change imperative for whole system reform.* Thousand Oaks: Corwin.

Fullan, M., & Quinn, J. (2016). *Coherence: The right drivers in action for schools, districts, and systems.* Thousand Oaks, CA: Corwin.

Garrett Dikkers, A., Whiteside, A. L., & Lewis, S. (2017). Blending face-to-face and online instruction to disrupt learning, inspire reflection, and create space for innovation. *In A. L. Whiteside, A. Garrett Dikkers, & K. Swan (Eds.), Social presence in online learning: Multiple perspectives on practice and research.* Sterling, VA: Stylus Publishing

Garrett Dikkers, A., Lewis, S., & Whiteside, A. L. (2015). Blended learning for students with disabilities: The North Carolina Virtual Public School's co-teaching model. *In M. F. Rice (Ed.), Exploring Pedagogies for Diverse Learners Online – Advances in Research on Teaching:* Vol. 25, 67-93.

Garrett Dikkers, Whiteside, A. L., & Tap, B. (2017). Social presence: Understanding connections among definitions, theory, measurements, and practice. *In A. L. Whiteside, A. Garrett Dikkers, & K. Swan (Eds.), Social presence in online learning: Multiple perspectives on practice and research.* Sterling, VA: Stylus Publishing.

GeoGuessr. (2020). *Let's explore the world!* Retrieved 15 June 2020, from https://www.geoguessr.com/

Harris, A. & Goodall, J. (2008). Do parents know they matter? Engaging all parents in learning. *Educational Research* 50(3), 277-289.

Hartman, H. J. (2001). *Metacognition in learning and instruction: Theory, research and practice.* Dordrecht: Kluwer Academic Publishers.

Hattie, J. (2012). *Visible learning for teachers: Maximizing impact on learning.*

Hillman, D. C., Willis, D. J., & Gunawardena, C. (1994). Learner-interface interaction in distance education: An extension of contemporary models and strategies for practitioners. *American Journal of Distance Education,*8(2), 30–42.

Institute of Education Sciences. (2008). *IES practice guide: Dropout prevention (NCEE 2008-4025).* Washington, DC: U.S. Department of Education.

In Hirumi, A. (2014). *Online and hybrid learning designs in action.*

Khan Academy. (2020). *About us.* Retrieved 15 June 2020, from https://www.khanacademy.org/about

Keeler, C. G., & Horney, M. (2007). Online course designs: Are special needs being met? *The American Journal of Distance Education,* 21(2): 61–75.

Keeler, C. G., Richter, J., Anderson-Inman, L., Horney, M. A., Ditson, M. (2007). Exceptional learners: Differentiated instruction online. *In C. Cavanaugh & R. Blomeyer (Eds.), What works in K-12 online learning* (pp. 125–178). Eugene, OR: International Society for Technology in Education

CSBA Blog. (2020). *Legislators, district administrators outline needs, goals to close the digital divide.* Retrieved 13 May 2020, from http://blog.csba.org/divide-taskforce/

Liu, F., & Cavanaugh, C. (2011). Success in online high school Biology: Factors influencing student academic performance. *Quarterly Review of Distance Education, 12*(1)

Loom. (2020). *About us.* Retrieved 15 June 2020, from https://www.loom.com/about-us

Lowes, S., Lin, P., & Kinghorn, B. (2015). Exploring the link between online behaviours and course performance in asynchronous online high school courses. *Journal of Learning Analytics, 2*(2), 169-194.

Margolis, A. R., Porter, A. L., & Pitterle, M. E. (2017). Best practices for use of blended learning. *American journal of pharmaceutical education, 81*(3), 49. https://doi.org/10.5688/ajpe81349

Morton, N. (2020). *The digital equity issues of confronting coronavirus with online education The Hechinger Report.* Retrieved 17 May 2020, from https://hechingerreport.org/should-schools-teach-anyone-who-can-get-online-or-no-one-at-all/

Padlet. (2020). *Features - Padlet.* Retrieved 15 June 2020, from https://padlet.com/premium/backpack

Pear Deck. (2020). *What are pear deck slides?* Retrieved 15 June 2020, from https://help.peardeck.com/what-are-pear-deck-slides

Pearson, D., Gallagher, M. (1983). The instruction of reading comprehension. *Contemporary Educational Psychology* 8(3) 317-344. doi:10.1016/0361-476X(83)900019-X.

Rose, R. M., & Blomeyer, R. L. (2007). *Access and equity in online classes and virtual schools. North American Council for Online Learning.* Vienna, VA: International Association for K–12 Online (iNACOL). Available online at http://www.nacol.org/docs/NACOL_EquityAccess.pdf.

Rose, D. H., & Gravel, J. W. (2010). *Technology and learning: Meeting special student's needs. National Center on Universal Design for Learning.* Retrieved from http://www.udlcenter. org/sites/udlcenter.org/files/TechnologyandLearning.pdf

ReadTheory. (2020). *About us.* Retrieved 15 June 2020, from https://readtheory.org/welcome/aboutUs?

Rice, M., & Dykman, B. (2018). The emerging research base for online learning and students with disabilities. *In R. Ferdig and K. Kennedy (Eds.) Handbook of research on K-12 online and blended learning* (pp. 189-206). Pittsburgh, PA: ETC Press

Jones, C. (2015). *10 reasons why teachers use Formative (goformative. com) — Community.* Retrieved 15 June 2020, from http://community.goformative.com/thoughts/2016/2/8/10-reasons-why-teachers-use-formative-goformativecom

Quizizz. (2020). *About us.* Retrieved 15 June 2020, from https://quizizz.com/about

San Diego County of Education. (2020). *Covid-19 planning assumptions.sdcoe.net.* Retrieved 13 May 2020, from https://covid-19.sdcoe.net/Portals/covid-19/Documents/Pandemic%20Plan%20Resources/20-04-14_Recovery_Plan_Assumptions_and_Recom

Screencastify. (2020). *Screencastify for education.* Retrieved 15 June 2020, from https://www.screencastify.com/education

Screencast-O-Matic. (2020). *Education screen recorder & video editor.* Retrieved 15 June 2020, from https://screencast-o-matic.com/education

Seale, C. (2020). *Distance Learning During The Coronavirus Pandemic: Equity And Access Questions For School Leaders. Forbes.* Retrieved 17 May 2020, from https://www.forbes.com/sites/colinseale/2020/03/17/distance-learning-during-the-coronavirus-pandemic-equity-and-access-questions-for-school-leaders/#dafee4e1d4d8

Smith, S. *(2016).* Invited In: Measuring UDL in online learning. *Center on Online Learning and Students with Disabilities.* Available from: http://centerononlinelearning.org/wp-content/uploads/InvitedIn4-18ALB.pdf

Snyder, K., Paska, L. M., & Besozzi, D. (2014). Cast from the past: Using screencasting in the social studies classroom. *The Social Studies*, 105(6), 310–314

Socrative. *(2020). About.* Retrieved 15 June 2020, from https://stg.socrative.com/

Steele, T. (2014). Use of KWLs in the online classroom as it correlates to increased participation. *Journal of Instructional Research*, 3, 8-14. Retrieved from https://eric.ed.gov/?id=EJ1127637

Swinson, J. (2012) Visible learning for teachers maximizing impact on learning, Educational Psychology in Practice, (28)2, 215-216, DOI: 10.1080/02667363.2012.693677

Tanujaya, B., & Mumu, J. (2019). Implementation of think-pair-share to mathematics instruction. *Journal of Education and Learning (EduLearn)*, 13(4), 510-517.

Time Magazine. (2020) *Superforecasters' are making eerily accurate predictions about COVID-19.* Retrieved 24 June 2020, from https://time.com/5848271/superforecaterscovid-19/

Tucker, C. R. (2019). *Blended learning in action + the on-your-feet: And, the on-your-feet guide to blended learning.* Thousand Oaks: Corwin.

Tucker, C. R. (2012). *Blended learning in grades 4-12: Leveraging the power of technology to create student-centered classrooms.* Thousand Oaks, Calif: Corwin.

U.S. Department of Education. (2020). *Questions and answers on providing services to children with disabilities during the coronavirus disease 2019 outbreak.* Retrieved 24 June 2020, from https://www2.ed.gov/policy/speced/guid/idea/memosdcltrs/qa-covid-19-03-12-2020.pdf

U.S. Department of Education. (2010). *Individualized, personalized, and differentiated instruction.* Retrieved from https://www.ed.gov/technology/draft-netp-2010/individualized-personalized-differentiated-instruction

U.S. Department of Education. (2017). Reimagining the role of technology in education. Office of Educational Technology. Retrieved from https://tech.ed.gov/files/2017/01/NETP17.pdf

U.S. Department of Education (2020). *Q&A in response to the inquiries concerning the implementation of IDEA Part B resolution procedures in the current COVID-19 environment.* Retrieved 24 June 2020, from https://www2.ed.gov/policy/speced/guid/idea/memosdcltrs/qa-dispute-resolution-procedures-part-b.pdf

Whiteboard Fox. (2020). *Whiteboard fox about.*Retrieved 15 June 2020, from https://whiteboardfox.com/

Wikpedia. (2020). *About*. Retrieved 15 June 2020, from https://en.wikipedia.org/wiki/Wikipedia:About

YoTeach!. (2020). *About and info*. Retrieved 15 June 2020, from http://palms.polyu.edu.hk/educational-apps/yoteach/

About the Author

Dr. Matthew Rhoads is an Educational Specialist, researcher, and writer. He received his Ed.D. in Educational Leadership from Concordia University, Irvine, his Masters in Teaching, and three teaching credentials (Mild to Moderate Education Specialist and English and Social Sciences Single Subject Credentials), and bachelors in Political Science from Point Loma Nazarene University. Dr. Rhoads has taught at the high school level in Mild to Moderate Special Education in the subjects English Language Arts, Social Sciences, and Math within inclusive co-taught classrooms and self-contained Special Education classrooms. In this role as a teacher and case manager, he utilized educational technology to create blended learning classrooms with an online component over the past five school years. Instructionally, he uses data to drive instructional decision-making in addition to employing elements of the universal design for learning to amplify his instruction to meet the needs of all of his students. During the spring of 2020, Dr. Rhoads conducted professional development and provided resources to move face to face mild/moderate classrooms to fully online distance learning classrooms in his district. Also, he has lectured to teacher candidates on incorporating edtech tools into classrooms while aligning best practice instructional strategies to be utilized along with the edtech. Dr. Rhoads has also had experience working at a start-up company that built a prototype student information system that focused on generating student data reports for Individualized Education Plans (IEP's) and Response to Intervention/Multiple Tier System of Supports (RTI/MTSS).

Dr. Rhoads research expertise relates to the efficacy of data practices among educational leaders as well as how educational leaders employ data practices and harness their leadership ability in establishing and participating in data-driven cultures in K-12 schools and districts. In addition, Dr. Rhoads has researched traditional and non-traditional professional development and its effectiveness in K-12 settings. He is currently a co-author of one book on Educational Technology for beginning teachers and has an active blog on educational technology and data. Dr. Rhoads has experience leading professional development on edtech tools and concurrent research-based instructional strategies at his school site, to university primary and secondary teacher candidates, and university faculty. On top of his teaching duties, Dr. Rhoads is a contributing member to the WASC, Edtech, PBIS, and School Site Council committees. For more information on Dr. Rhoads, access to his blog, and his other publications, go to www.matthewrhoads.com.

Expertise

Education Data Techniques/Practices and Applications, Teacher and Educational Leader Data-Driven Decision Making, Edtech Tools and Instruction, Professional Development Best Practices, School Improvement & Systems Thinking, and Special Education.

Hobbies/Personal Life

In his free time, Dr. Rhoads loves playing and watching basketball, working out and being active, going out to new restaurants, and traveling while spending time with his wife and puppy.

Made in the USA
San Bernardino, CA
14 July 2020